She Called Me Her Sweet Girl

A Legacy of Life Lessons to Live Well and Thrive

Crystal Wheeler

Sweet Lilly Girl Publications

Leesburg, Va

Crystal Wheeler/Sweet Lilly Girl Publications

Website: https://www.blissfulbalancelifecoaching.com

Email: info@blissfulbalancelifecoaching.com

Ordering Information:

Quantity Sales. Special discounts are available on quantity purchases by corporations, associations, and others. For details, contact the publisher at the address above.

She Called Me Her Sweet Girl: A Legacy of Life Lessons to Live Well and Thrive/ Crystal Wheeler /1st.ed.

ISBN 979-8-9911648-0-1 Paperback

ISBN 979-8-9911648-1-8 eBook

DEDICATION

I dedicate this book to my loving Grandmother, Vernesta Brady Lilly, who called me her sweet girl. She saw in me a bright future and all the possibilities that I could ever imagine. She was my rock and walking book of wisdom. She lived a life full of grace, hope, and love. I never saw her get angry or speak an ill word toward anyone. I miss her immensely and strive to be like her every day.

My Grandmother passed away before I was able to finish this book, which seeks to capture the true essence of living by faith and loving God. I dedicate this book to her undeniable legacy—a legacy of love, pure excellence, unwavering faith, and resilience. She always reminded me to keep God first in my life and often expressed how proud she was of me.

As with any great teacher, she will live eternally in those who knew and loved her. This is her book, and I am always honored to be called her Sweet Girl.

ACKNOWLEDGMENTS

First and foremost, thank you, Heavenly Father, for instilling a profound love for reading and writing in my seven-year-old spirit. Your guidance has been my anchor throughout this journey, and I am eternally grateful for Your presence in my life.

A heartfelt thank you to Linda Griffin for believing in me from the very beginning. Your faith in my abilities has been a cornerstone of my success, and your support has been invaluable.

To those who loved on me throughout this process, your support has been irreplaceable. Thank you to my core group, whose continuous inspiration encouraged me to share my story and that of my grandmother. Your encouragement has been a constant source of motivation and strength.

To my amazing children, Miles and Morgan, thank you for allowing Mom the space and time to write and, most of all, for cheering me on when I doubted my ability to finish. Morgan, your sweet reminders to stay encouraged and push through have been my lifeline. Miles, your cool, calm, and collected demeanor taught me not to stress and to keep cool. You both are my greatest blessings and my source of strength.

To my mother, Deloris, thank you for teaching me the true essence of being an advocate and the greatest cheerleader for my children. Your example has shaped me in ways words cannot fully express. To my father, thank you for the life lessons of not taking NO for an answer and for encouraging me to question and understand the intent behind my actions.

To Veronica Harris, my first track coach and mentor, thank you for pushing me beyond my limits. Your belief in me has been instrumental.

Numerous amazing people have contributed in countless ways to my experiences in capturing the true essence of this book. To all of you, I extend my deepest gratitude. Your contributions, whether big or small, have made this journey possible and this book a reality. I want to especially thank Andrea "Krissie" Johnson, Sacquana Frierson Leathers, Kimberly Scott, Marlena Pickens Young, Dr. Alonda Alloway, Dr. Sonya Greene, and Lauren Williams Berty. Thank you all for being a part of this journey with me. Your belief in me and your unwavering support have made all the difference. This book is a testament to the power of faith, love, and the incredible impact of a supportive community.

Table of Contents

INTRODUCTION

I wrote this book to honor my Grandmother Vernesta, a woman of immense faith and grace whose life and legacy have profoundly shaped who I am today. Her story is not just a personal tale of triumph and resilience but a testament to the power of faith, wisdom, and unwavering strength. Grandmother Vernesta was a remarkable woman whose influence extended far beyond her immediate family, touching the lives of everyone who had the privilege of knowing her.

In my formative years, I was fortunate to spend a great deal of time with my grandmother. She was a living repository of wisdom and life lessons, a blueprint for how to live a wholesome and meaningful life. Her teachings were far more impactful than anything I could have learned from a book. She taught me the importance of faith, the value of grace, and the power of resilience. Through her actions and words, she demonstrated how to navigate life's challenges with dignity and strength. Her faith was her guiding light, and she imparted this same sense of spiritual grounding to me.

Grandmother Vernesta's life story is a remarkable one, filled with experiences that deserve to be shared with the world. She lived through times of great change and hardship, yet she always remained steadfast in her beliefs and values. Her journey was one of perseverance and hope, and her ability to find joy and purpose in every situation was truly inspiring. By sharing her story, I aim to honor her memory and ensure that her legacy lives on for future generations to learn from and be inspired by.

Writing this book was also a deeply personal journey for me. It was an opportunity to reflect on the countless ways my grandmother influenced my life and shaped my character. Her teachings were not just about surviving but thriving and finding beauty and purpose in everyday moments. She showed me how to be strong in the face of adversity, how to maintain my faith even when things seemed impossible, and how to treat others with kindness and compassion. These lessons have been invaluable to me, and I believe they can offer the same guidance and inspiration to others.

Grandmother Vernesta's story is also a reminder of the importance of honoring our roots and cherishing the wisdom of our elders. In today's fast-paced world, we often overlook the invaluable knowledge and experiences that older generations have to offer. By documenting and sharing her story, I hope to highlight the enduring relevance of her teachings and the universal truths they convey.

Moreover, this book is a tribute to the enduring bond between a grandparent and a grandchild. The relationship I had with my grandmother was one of the most significant and enriching connections of my life. She was not just a family member but a mentor, a confidante, and a source of unwavering support. Writing this book is my way of expressing my gratitude for everything she taught me and the love she gave so freely.

In conclusion, I wrote this book to honor my Grandmother Vernesta because her life was a beacon of faith, grace, and wisdom. She was the blueprint for living a meaningful and wholesome life, and her remarkable story deserves to be shared. Through this book, I aim to preserve her legacy, share her invaluable lessons with others, and celebrate her profound impact on my life and the lives of many others.

The First Lesson: Keep Living

He heals the brokenhearted and binds up their wounds.

— (PSALMS 147:3 NIV)

On January 16, 2020, at 12:38 a.m., my life changed forever. I watched my Grandmother Vernesta take her last breath. I sang to her one of her favorite songs as she labored through her final moments. The lyrics of the song filled the room: "What a mighty God we serve, what a mighty God we serve. Angels bow before Him, heaven and earth adore Him, what a mighty God we serve."

She was staring at me as she inhaled and exhaled rapidly. Through my tears, I whispered, "It's okay, Ma, we will be okay. I will be okay." I was sitting on the floor and began to pray. I knew that life was going to change. I had never felt that kind of pain before.

I went to work the next morning, feeling like a shadow of myself. By 9:00 am, I received a phone call telling me to come home immediately. My initial plan was to go home on the weekend, but my mother and family needed me right away. When I arrived, my mother relinquished her role

Vernesta Brady Lilly otherwise known as Ma

to me to execute the arrangements for my grandmother. I met with the ministers, pastor, and church members. I worked with the funeral director on the details of the service. It felt like an out-of-body experience, but it wasn't—it was one of spiritual duty. I didn't have the opportunity to grieve properly.

I somehow became responsible for officiating the service. In the days following my grandmother's death, I found myself lost in a whirlwind of emotions and responsibilities. I coordinated with relatives traveling in from out of town, managed the influx of condolences, and ensured every detail of the service was perfect. Through it all, I felt a profound sense of duty to honor my grandmother's memory. She had always been a pillar of the community, known for her kindness and unwavering faith. It was only fitting that her farewell reflected the same grace and dignity she embodied.

As I navigated through these challenging days, memories of my grandmother flooded my mind. I recalled the countless times she had shared her wisdom with me, her laughter, and the warmth of her embrace. She had a way of making everyone feel special, of imparting a sense of belonging. Her home had always been a sanctuary, a place where love and faith intertwined seamlessly.

The night she passed away, as I sang to her and held her hand, I felt a profound connection to her spirit. It was as if she was passing on her strength and faith to me in her final moments. Her eyes, filled with a mixture of pain and peace, seemed to convey a message of reassurance. "You are ready," they seemed to say. "You will carry on."

My five-year-old daughter sang beautifully during the service as she honored her great-grandmother. Something she would do for her when she visited. At one point in the service, the pastor turned to me and said, "Sister Lilly's legacy must continue. You must witness and share the testimony of Jesus' good news." His words echoed in my mind, adding weight to the already heavy burden of loss I carried. My Grandmother had been the matriarch of our family, a beacon of strength and faith. Her passing left a void that seemed impossible to fill.

The days turned into weeks, and the initial shock of her passing began to wear off, replaced by a deep, persistent ache. I missed her terribly. The reality of her absence hit me hardest in the quiet moments—when I would instinctively reach for the phone to call her, only to remember she was no longer there. In those moments, I felt an overwhelming sense of loss, a void that seemed impossible to fill.

But amidst the grief, I also felt a growing sense of purpose. The pastor's words during the service planted a seed in my heart. My Grandmother's legacy was not just about remembering her life; it was about continuing her mission. She had lived a life of service and faith, always putting others before herself. She had dedicated her life to spreading the message of God's love and grace. Now, it was my turn to carry that torch.

One particular story stood out to me. A young woman approached me after a service, tears streaming down her face. She told me how my grandmother had helped her during a difficult time, offering not just words of comfort but also tangible support. "She gave me hope when I had none," the woman said. "She saved my life." Hearing these words filled me with a renewed sense of purpose. My Grandmother's legacy was not just a memory; it was a living, breathing testament to the power of faith and love.

As I continued my journey, I began to see signs of my grandmother's presence everywhere. A particularly beautiful sunrise, the sound of her favorite hymn playing on the radio, the unexpected kindness of a stranger—all these moments felt like reminders that she was still with me, guiding me. I started to write down these experiences, creating a journal of memories and reflections. This became a source of comfort and strength, a way to process my grief and celebrate her life.

One day, while reading through my journal, I came across the lyrics of the song I had sung to her on her final night: "What a mighty God we serve, what a mighty God we serve. Angels bow before Him, heaven and earth adore Him, what a mighty God we serve." The words resonated deeply, reminding me of the faith that had sustained my grandmother throughout her life. I decided to share these reflections with the church community, hoping to inspire others as my grandmother had inspired me.

I spoke at a Sunday service, sharing my journey of loss and faith and the profound impact my grandmother had on my life. I talked about the night she passed away, the song I had sung, and the pastor's words about continuing her legacy. I shared the stories from my journal, the moments that had brought me closer to her spirit. As I spoke, I saw tears in the eyes of the congregation, a collective sense of shared grief and hope.

After the service, many people approached me, expressing gratitude and sharing their stories of loss and faith. It was a deeply moving experience, one that reinforced my belief in the importance of community and the power of sharing our stories. My Grandmother had always believed in the strength of the human spirit and the ability to find light even in the darkest times. I realized that by sharing my journey, I was not only honoring her memory but also helping others find their own strength and faith.

The process of healing was slow, and there were days when the pain of her absence felt unbearable. But through my faith and the support of my community, I found the strength to carry on. My Grandmother had taught me that life was a journey of love, service, and faith. Even in her absence, she continued to guide me, her legacy shaping my actions and beliefs.

In the end, I realized that grief and loss are not just about mourning the absence of a loved one but also about celebrating their life and the impact they had on the world. My Grandmother's passing was a turning point in my life, a moment that changed everything. But it also became a source of strength and inspiration, a reminder of the power of love and faith.

As I look back on that night, the memory of her final moments is no longer just a source of pain but also of peace. I know she is in a better place, her spirit free and at peace. And I carry her legacy with me, a beacon of light guiding me through the challenges and joys of life. She taught me that even in the face of loss, we can find strength and hope. Her life was a testament to the power of faith, and her legacy continues to inspire and uplift those who knew her.

Grandma Vernesta's words of wisdom on losing a loved one:
"You have to keep living. We all will go see the Lord one day, but in the meantime, you have to keep living.

Reflect on Your Grief Journey:

- Have you ever experienced grief? If so, what memories do you cherish with the person you've lost? Write about a particularly joyful moment you shared.

- What coping mechanisms have you tried? Which ones have been helpful, and which ones haven't?

- How can you incorporate the lessons and values of your loved one into your life moving forward?

- What are some ways you can take care of yourself physically, emotionally, and spiritually as you continue to grieve?

CHAPTER

02

You Can Make
It if You Try

Let us not become weary in doing good,
for at the proper time we will reap
a harvest if we do not give up.

– (GALATIANS 6:9 NIV)

"You can make it if you try." These words resonate deeply within me, echoing the relentless spirit of my grandmother, a woman who, despite facing overwhelming hardships, never surrendered to despair. Instead, she chose to push forward, praying with unwavering faith and relentlessly pursuing a better life. Her journey is a testament to the power of determination and faith, teaching us that hope and perseverance can lead us to brighter days, even in the darkest times.

The fatal house fire that left six loved ones dead seemed too much to bear for one person. In the wake of losing half her family, my grandmother could have succumbed to sorrow and hopelessness. Such a devastating loss would cripple many, yet she was determined to live and thrive. Her resilience became a beacon of hope for those around her, illuminating the path of perseverance and courage. Her story is not just one of survival but of triumph over adversity.

"Trying indicates you have enough inside you to make the effort." This profound statement captures the essence of my grandmother's approach to life. She believed that making an effort, no matter how small, was a sign of inner strength and potential. Effort, to her, was not merely about the physical act but also about having faith in oneself and in God's plan. If you don't make the effort, you won't know the outcome. This simple yet powerful philosophy drove her to keep pushing forward, regardless of the obstacles in her path.

Walter Mack Lilly |

With only an 8th-grade education, my grandmother was never ashamed of her academic limitations. Instead, she embraced them, proudly sharing her story to inspire others. Her wisdom transcended formal education; it was rooted in lived experiences and a deep, unwavering faith in God. "She was wiser than most because she lived her life by Godly wisdom," a truth evident in her actions and the legacy she left behind.

One of her guiding principles was to prioritize essential needs and trust in divine provision. She often said, "If you make sure you have a roof over your head, pay your bills, and tithe, God will take care of the rest." This statement encapsulated her belief in practical faith—taking care of one's responsibilities while trusting God to handle the rest. It wasn't just advice but a way of life that she demonstrated daily.

Her life was a vivid illustration of digging deep to desire better than what you have. This internal drive propelled her forward, motivating her to achieve more than seemed possible. Despite the numerous challenges she faced, she never stopped striving for a better future for herself and her family. Her determination was not just about achieving personal success but also about lifting others and setting an example of what is possible with faith and effort.

The power of prayer was central to her resilience. My Grandmother prayed with the conviction that her prayers would be answered, believing firmly in the power of divine intervention. This faith was not passive but active, intertwined with her relentless efforts to improve her situation. She believed that prayer and action went hand in hand; one without the other was incomplete.

Her ability to persevere and remain hopeful in the face of adversity has been a guiding light in my own life. Whenever I face challenges, I remember her words and her example. She taught me that faith and effort are inseparable, that you must pray as if everything depends on God and work as if everything depends on you. My Grandmother knew how to manage multiple tasks well. Her time management skills were impeccable. This balanced approach to life has been a source of strength for me, helping me navigate through my own trials.

One of the most significant lessons she imparted was the importance of community and support. She understood that no one could make it alone, and she actively sought to build and nurture relationships with those around her. Her home was always open to others, and she was quick to offer help, advice, or a kind word to anyone in need. This sense of community, built on mutual support and shared faith, was a cornerstone of her life and a key element of her resilience.

In reflecting on her life, I am reminded that determination and faith are not abstract concepts but practical tools we can use to navigate our journeys. Her story teaches us that no matter how dire our circumstances are, we have within us the strength to push forward, make the effort, and have faith in the outcome. It is a reminder that even the smallest act of trying can set us on a path to change and improvement.

Her legacy lives on in the lives of those she touched, a testament to the enduring power of faith and effort. She showed that you don't need formal education to be wise, that you don't need wealth to be rich in spirit, and that you don't need a perfect life to inspire others. Her life was a masterpiece of resilience, painted with strokes of faith, effort, and unwavering determination.

It has always been my belief that if you were obedient, followed God's word, and did as you were told, your life would be semi-perfect. At least you would get what you wanted. I thought if I didn't seek popularity and chart my own path, life would be good for me. What I had not expected was that I would be heartbroken on my knees, trying to figure out what I had possibly done to deserve to be landed in an awful place, questioning why.

Before graduating high school, I had a goal to compete in the Olympics. I played basketball and ran track throughout high school. I also knew that I was going to go to college. From the time I was old enough to pick up a book, my mother poured into my siblings and me that we were to get an education. In my spirit, I always knew that I was destined for greatness. Living in North Carolina forever was not in my cards, and I knew I was going somewhere.

In the summer of my junior year of high school, I worked out every day and competed in summer track, hoping to receive a full ride to attend college. I always had a plan B. During my senior year, I was completing college applications. I recall walking into the guidance counselor's office to get a college application for several schools. I had been in contact with a few track coaches but needed to complete the college applications.

One of the more popular girls in school walked in before me and was greeted with several pleasantries. She requested the college applications and was provided with each one she asked for. I greeted the counselor with a smile, and as I was requesting an application, she handed me an application for the local community college. I paused with a puzzled look and shook my head as if to say no, that's not the application I requested. She was looking equally puzzled and insulted. I declined the community college application and told her that I would like the same college application she had just handed to the student who had just walked out. I couldn't understand why she would not extend the same courtesy to me as she did to the other student.

I remember walking out feeling angry and just completely disappointed. There was something that caused her to discount me. I began to rattle off in my head all my student involvement; I was on the honor roll, a student-athlete, and an overall well-rounded student. However, somehow, the academic counselor was inclined to give me an application for a two-year technical college. I knew I could be so much more and wanted to compete in track and field at the collegiate level. I knew at that moment I would not have my future determined by someone else's opinion.

My Grandmother's life is a powerful reminder that you can make it if you try. Her life story teaches us that we have the power to overcome them. By pushing and praying until we see something different, by digging deep to want better than what we have, and by living a life guided by Godly wisdom, we can achieve more than we ever thought possible. Her legacy is a testament to the human spirit's capacity to rise above adversity, strive for a better future, and inspire others to do the same.

Grandma Vernesta's Wisdom on Trying:
"Put forth the effort, and God will take care of the rest. You don't know what you are capable of if you don't try. Even when you are scared, try anyway."

Reflect on Your Journey for Giving Your Best Effort:

- What are your main goals right now? Why are they important to you?
- What motivates you to keep trying, even when things get tough?
- List three things you have accomplished recently, no matter how small. How do these accomplishments make you feel?
- Who or what in your life inspires you to keep going? How can you draw strength from them?
- List three specific, achievable goals you can set for the next week. How will you track your progress?

Act Like You Already Have It

*For I know the plans I have for you," declares
the Lord, "plans to prosper you and not to harm
you, plans to give you hope and a future."*

− (JEREMIAH 29:11 NIV)

There is much to be said about the power of manifesting, visualizing, and having faith. Believing in your capabilities and envisioning success can be a powerful motivator. This was some of the best advice my grandma gave to me. It was pure, unadulterated wisdom. Except for the Bible, there was no book that she read that she gained this wisdom.

I had always been a dreamer or visionary. I often shared my hopes and dreams with her. My heart believed that I could have anything and be anything. Acting as if I already possessed the things I wanted, qualities, and accomplishments were my focus. I thought for sure that if I kept my mindset, things would fall in line easily.

As I matured, one of my desires was to be a wife. I believed that I would marry a wonderful man and create my own family. I thought that keeping this mindset would help me with my decision-making. She often said, "Act like you already have it." "Act like you're already a wife." "If it's what you want, believe it." She would also tell me to read Mark, "Therefore I tell you, whatever you ask for in prayer, believe that you have received it, and it will be yours," (Mark 11:24 NIV). "Pray and have faith it will be yours," she would often say.

I couldn't for the life of me understand why she was so confident. Her faith seemed so unshakable. I think that is why I had such a difficult time when it seemed I made all the right decisions, and the outcomes didn't align. At least, I thought they were misaligned. Somehow, I found myself faced with a load of responsibilities that I did not believe I could physically and mentally handle. I was all alone in Northern Virginia with no family support and a booming career. The demands of being a mother and increasing responsibility at work seemed to put me in what I called a crazy cycle. I was not resting and would burn both ends of the candle. My Grandmother told me to believe, she told me to read the scripture, and she told me to have a positive mindset. I did all of that, so what was going on? I still felt overwhelmed.

This situation became more of a test of my mental stamina. My mind would race on what it is that I knew I needed to do to stop the crazy cycle. I wanted peace. I knew that if I wanted peace, I would have to do something different than what I was doing. I was approaching my 40th birthday and remember telling God I couldn't live the way I was. I was so unhappy and fearful. Fearful that I would die unhappy. Fearful that I had lost myself, I didn't know if I would return. I had to accept and embrace the fact that this was the life I was living. For years, I lived and breathed these actions and words, only to see that no matter how committed I was to these beliefs, it didn't guarantee the outcome I wanted and the way I wanted it.

Every morning, I would always pray, but I knew it would take more than prayer to keep me going. I began a daily ritual, which I continue today, by looking into the mirror and reciting the affirmations I need to hear. "I am bold, I am powerful, I am resilient, this is temporary, better is coming, I am love, I am loving, I am worthy, I am deserving. I also became more intentional about my health. I worked out twice a day to manage my own stress levels. I identified areas in my life that did not serve me well. I only focused on activities that made me happy, people who were positive and wanted good for me.

There were times when it was difficult. When I would start to cry, I would remind myself that the tears were temporary, and I was not built to break. This was growth and experience that helped me understand that I was, in fact, getting exactly what I had prayed and hoped for. Acting as if I already possessed what I desired would manifest it. I just needed to trust my abilities, stay focused on my goals, and maintain a resilient mindset. I didn't give up. I kept believing and hoping. I learned that maintaining a positive outlook, even in challenging times, can help you build resilience and perspective. I remembered that God gave me everything I needed. The setbacks can help pave the way for new opportunities and growth. I learned to express gratitude for what I have and even what I did not have. I focused on the lessons that I had learned along the way.

My positive attitude had opened so many more doors that I had not even considered. Cultivating a positive mindset can help you navigate through difficult times with grace and optimism. By focusing on solutions rather than dwelling on problems, you can discover new opportunities and creative ways to overcome obstacles. Remember that your attitude plays a crucial role in shaping your experiences, and by staying positive, you can find the strength to persevere and achieve your goals, no matter how tough the situations may seem.

Your attitude can significantly impact how you perceive and respond to the world around you. By approaching life with a positive mindset, you can overcome any obstacle. Your attitude is within your control, and choosing a positive outlook can substantially affect how you experience life's ups and downs. Your attitude influences your actions and decisions. I learned that even though the days were long and nights dark, I had to persevere, and the darkness was temporary. I forgave myself for allowing the darkness to stay longer than I wanted it to. My faith had been tested to the point where I had no other option but to have faith.

I had to keep reminding myself that God would come through for me. God is working. He does what he says he will do. My faith was being tested, but everyone's is. I was determined to pass this test. Believing that what you desire is already yours can be a powerful mindset that can help you manifest your goals and aspirations. Embracing this belief can strengthen your determination and commitment, leading you to take actions that align with your vision. Maintaining a positive attitude and staying focused on your objectives can attract the necessary resources and opportunities to turn your aspirations into reality. By visualizing your success and consistently affirming your belief in achieving your goals, you can reinforce your determination and resilience to make your dreams a reality.

JoAnn Lilly Age Two

Keeping a positive mindset helped me rise above negativity and adversity. I focused on nurturing all good things, such as optimism and resilience. Things that were true. I often meditated on Philippians, "Finally, brothers and sisters, whatever is true, whatever is noble, whatever is right, whatever is pure, whatever is lovely, whatever is admirable—if anything is excellent or praiseworthy—think about such things." (Philippians 4:8 NIV) My Grandmother was a positive thinker and encouraged all of us to be the same way. Don't ever stop thinking about what is truly worthwhile and worthy of praise. I had to remind myself that these were instructions from God. This mindset helped me to focus on solutions rather than dwell on the problems that I faced. Trust your abilities and keep moving forward with confidence and conviction.

Grandma Vernesta's Words of Wisdom on Believing:

"Whatever it is you want, pray about it and believe it is yours. If you want a new car, see yourself driving the new car. If you want to be a wife, act like you are already where you want to be. "

Reflect on Your Journey Believing for What You Desire:

- What are your deepest desires and dreams? Write them down in detail.

- Why are these desires important to you? How will achieving them impact your life?

- How do you define faith and trust in the context of achieving your desires?

- How can you create a plan or roadmap to achieve your goals? Break it down into manageable tasks.

- How can you align your daily actions and decisions with your heart's desires?

Let Go and Let God

Come to me, all you who are weary and burdened, and I will give you rest. Take my yoke upon you and learn from me, for I am gentle and humble in heart, and you will find rest for your souls. For my yoke is easy and my burden is light.

— (MATTHEW 11:28-30 NIV)

Refusing to hold a grudge is a powerful act of self-preservation. Clinging to resentment is like sipping poison, expecting the other person to suffer. In reality, it corrodes your spirit, clouding the clarity of your emotions and poisoning the well-being of your soul. When you harbor grudges, you're not just retaining the memory of an offense; you're allowing it to fester and spread, affecting your outlook on life. The poison seeps into your thoughts, tainting your perceptions and coloring your interactions. It becomes a heavy burden weighing down your spirit with negativity. Choosing to let go is a conscious decision to break free from this toxic cycle. It's an acknowledgment that your peace of mind is more valuable than holding onto past grievances.

Shirley Ann Lilly Age 3

By releasing the grip of resentment, you create a space for healing and growth. The energy once consumed by anger and bitterness can now be redirected toward positive endeavors and personal development. In the absence of grudges, your spirit can breathe freely, unburdened by the weight of negativity. Forgiveness becomes a balm for your soul, fostering a sense of inner harmony. So, resist holding grudges. It is a poison that only harms your spirit. Choose the path to forgiveness and watch your spirit blossom in the light of a newfound freedom.

This may seem too hard to do when someone blatantly harms you. The invaluable lessons stick with me today. Life's trials often feel overwhelming, and the urge to take matters into our own hands can be powerful. However, we are reminded in 2 Chronicles that we do not have to face these battles alone: "Do not be afraid or discouraged because of this vast army. For the battle is not yours, but God's." (2 Chronicles 20:15 NIV) This profound scripture teaches us to trust God's power and justice, even when faced with the most personal and painful conflicts.

God will fight your battles, even those you want to fight. When we encounter injustices, particularly those that hurt us deeply, our natural response may be to seek retribution. Yet, scripture encourages us to let God deal with the vengeance. Romans states, "Do not take revenge, my dear friends, but leave room for God's wrath, for it is written: "It is mine to avenge; I will repay," says the Lord. (Romans 12:19 NIV)

Holding onto anger and grudges can be incredibly damaging to our own well-being. When your heart is pure and not holding on to the weight of a grudge, it gives you power. It frees you from the chains of bitterness and allows you to focus on the positive aspects of your life. Forgiveness does not mean excusing harmful behavior, but it does mean releasing yourself from the burden of anger and resentment.

The concept of divine justice is central to the Christian faith. Trusting that God will fight our battles and deliver justice in His time is a powerful form of faith. It requires us to surrender our desire for immediate retribution and trust that God's plan is greater than our own. In my situation, I had to believe that God's justice would prevail, even if I didn't see it immediately. This belief helped me stay focused on my responsibilities and children rather than getting entangled in a cycle of vengeance and negativity.

Over time, I witnessed God's hand at work, not just in my life but also in the subtle shifts in circumstances that aligned with His will. When faced with challenges that seem insurmountable, it is comforting to remember that the battle is not yours but God's. This perspective shift can alleviate a great deal of stress and anxiety. It reminds us that we are not alone and do not have to carry the weight of our struggles by ourselves. Trusting that God was fighting for me allowed me to sleep at night and approach each day with renewed hope.

Trusting God to fight our battles involves both spiritual and practical steps. Spend time in prayer, asking God to help you release your anger and trust in His justice. Meditation on scriptures that affirm God's power and justice can also reinforce your faith. Actively work on forgiving those who have wronged you. This doesn't mean excusing their behavior but choosing to let go of the bitterness that can consume your heart. Lean on your faith community for support. Share your struggles with trusted friends or a spiritual advisor who can pray with you and offer encouragement. Continue to fulfill your responsibilities, especially those that pertain to your family and personal well-being.

Trust that God will provide the strength and resources you need. We are empowered to persevere through adversity when we trust that God will fight our battles. The journey of trusting God to fight your battles is ongoing. It involves continual surrender and faith in His plan. As we move forward, it's important to maintain this trust and stay open to the ways God is working in our lives. One of the most profound realizations I've had is that God often works in ways we do not expect.

God's promise to fight our battles extends to all areas of our lives. Whether we are dealing with personal conflicts, professional challenges, or societal injustices, we can trust that God is with us. This trust does not mean passivity; it means active faith and reliance on God's power. In practical terms, this means making decisions that align with our faith and values, even when faced with opposition. It means speaking the truth and acting justly, knowing that God is our ultimate defender.

Letting go of the desire for personal vengeance is not a sign of weakness but a demonstration of strength and faith. It shows that we trust in a higher power to deliver justice and that we are not bound by the actions of others. For me, letting go involved acknowledging the pain I experienced while choosing to focus on my own growth and healing. It meant trusting that God saw my struggles and would act in His time. This act of letting go was liberating and empowering. Life's battles can be daunting, especially when they involve deep personal pain and betrayal. However, we can find peace and strength by trusting in God's justice and letting go of the desire for personal vengeance.

In all circumstances, remember that the battle is not yours but God's. Trust in His power and justice and let go of the desire for personal retribution. By doing so, we align ourselves with God's greater plan and find true peace and strength.

Grandma Vernesta's Words of Wisdom about Letting Go:
*"Give it to God, He will handle it. He will
never leave you or forsake you."*

Reflect on Your Journey for Letting God fight your battles:

- What does "letting go and letting God" mean to you personally?

- In what areas of your life do you struggle with control or have difficulty letting go?

- How can you practice surrendering small things in your daily life as a step towards letting go of bigger concerns?

- How do you envision your life changing if you fully embrace the practice of letting go and letting God?

- Describe a situation where you successfully let go and trusted in a higher power. What was the outcome?

Take Care of Yourself

*For physical training is of some
value, but godliness has value for all
things, holding promise for both the
present life and the life to come.*

– (1 TIMOTHY 4:8 NIV)

My Grandmother Vernesta was a remarkable woman whose life was a testament to the principles of faith, grace, and holistic self-care. She understood the importance of nurturing both the mind and body long before the term "self-care" became a popular concept. Throughout her life, she practiced self-care with a level of dedication and discipline that has always inspired me. Her approach to self-care was comprehensive and deeply rooted in her faith, reflecting her belief that caring for the body was as important as nurturing the soul.

*Vernesta Brady Lilly at
her Sons funeral*

Grandmother Vernesta had a routine that she followed with unwavering commitment. She believed in the power of movement and exercise to maintain her physical health. Every morning, she would go for a walk, taking in the fresh air and appreciating the beauty of nature. Those walks weren't very far, but she ensured she would move her body. Her walks were not just a form of exercise but also a time for reflection and prayer. She often said, "I pray, but I got to take care of this body of mine. God gave us one body, and we must take care of it." This mantra guided her daily actions and was a lesson she imparted to everyone around her.

In addition to walking, she regularly rode her exercise bike. She understood the benefits of cardiovascular exercise long before it became a common fitness recommendation. Riding her exercise bike was a way to keep her heart healthy and her body strong. She would often pedal away while listening to gospel stations on television, combining her love for physical activity with her spiritual practices. This blend of physical exercise and spiritual nourishment was a hallmark of her self-care routine.

Stretching was another essential part of her daily regimen. She would gently stretch her muscles every morning and evening, ensuring that her body remained flexible and free from stiffness. She believed that stretching was crucial for maintaining mobility and preventing injuries. Her stretching routine was almost meditative, a quiet time where she could connect with her body and prepare herself for the day ahead or unwind before bed.

Grandmother Vernesta's approach to self-care extended beyond physical health. She was a firm believer in the importance of mental and emotional well-being. She often emphasized that "We have to take care of both our mind and body. Overall wellness is not optional." She practiced mindfulness and meditation through prayer, finding solace and strength in her faith. Her prayers were heartfelt conversations with God, through which she sought guidance, expressed gratitude, and found peace. This spiritual practice was her way of maintaining mental clarity and emotional stability, allowing her to navigate life's challenges with grace and resilience.

Her home was a sanctuary of peace and positivity. She created a space where tranquility and comfort were paramount. Fresh flowers often adorned her living room, and the scent of homemade meals filled the air, creating a nurturing and uplifting environment. She believed that a clean, organized, and beautiful living space was essential for mental well-being.

Her home reflected her inner calm and was a place where family and friends felt welcomed and loved.

Grandmother Vernesta also believed in the power of nutrition for maintaining overall health. She was mindful of the foods she consumed, understanding that a balanced diet was crucial for physical vitality. Her meals were simple yet nutritious, often featuring fresh fruits, vegetables, and whole grains. She avoided processed foods and sugary snacks, preferring instead to eat what she called "God's food" – natural, wholesome ingredients that nourished her body. She would often remind us that "You are what you eat," a saying that highlighted her belief in the connection between diet and health.

Her dedication to self-care was not just about maintaining her own well-being but also about setting an example for her family and community. She believed that by taking care of herself, she was better equipped to take care of others. Her actions demonstrated that self-care was not selfish but a necessary foundation for a life of service and compassion. She was always there to offer support and guidance to those in need, whether through a listening ear, a comforting meal, or a wise piece of advice. Her ability to care for others so profoundly was rooted in her practice of taking care of herself.

One of the most profound lessons I learned from Grandmother Vernesta was the importance of balance. She understood that wellness was not about perfection but about finding harmony between the different aspects of life. She balanced her physical activities with rest, her spiritual practices with everyday responsibilities, and her personal needs with the needs of others. This sense of balance allowed her to live a fulfilling and meaningful life, one that was rich in love, joy, and purpose.

In today's fast-paced world, my grandmother's life lessons are more relevant than ever. Many people struggle to find time for self-care, often prioritizing work and other obligations over their own health and well-being. However, Grandmother Vernesta's life reminds us that self-care is not a luxury but a necessity. It is an essential practice that enables us to live our best lives and to be our best selves for those we love and care for.

Writing this book to honor my Grandmother Vernesta is my way of preserving and sharing the wisdom she imparted to me. Her story is a powerful reminder that true wellness encompasses both the mind and body and that taking care of ourselves is an act of respect for the life and body we have been given. Her teachings have had a lasting impact on my life, guiding me in my journey of self-care and overall wellness.

My Grandmother's life was a masterclass in holistic self-care. Her daily practices of walking, riding her exercise bike, and stretching were more than just routines; they were expressions of her belief in the importance of maintaining physical health. Her emphasis on mental and emotional well-being through prayer and creating a peaceful home environment demonstrated her understanding of the interconnectedness of mind and body. Her mindful approach to nutrition and ability to balance various aspects of life provided a blueprint for living wholesomely. By sharing her remarkable story, I hope to inspire others to embrace self-care as a fundamental part of their lives, just as she did. Grandmother Vernesta's legacy is one of faith, grace, and the unwavering belief that overall wellness is not optional but essential.

I knew that to take care of myself and have a long, healthy life, I had to implement my own self-care plan. My top priorities were the big three, as I call them: mental, spiritual, and physical health. Caring for my overall well-being would require a holistic approach that nurtured my mental, physical, and spiritual health. I want to share with you my strategies for making these steps part of my lifestyle that you can also consider:

1. **Mental Health:**

    a. Therapy and Counseling: Engage in regular sessions with a mental health professional to explore and address your thoughts, emotions, and challenges.

    b. Mindfulness and Meditation: Practice mindfulness to cultivate a present-focused awareness and consider incorporating meditation into your routine to promote mental clarity.

    c. Hobbies and Creative Outlets: Pursue activities that bring you joy and satisfaction, whether it's art, music, writing, or any other creative expression.

2. **Physical Health:**

    a. Regular Exercise: Establish a fitness routine that suits your preferences, whether it's cardio, strength training, yoga, or a combination. Physical activity contributes not only to your physical health but also boosts your mood.

b. Balanced Nutrition: Maintain a well-balanced diet rich in fruits, vegetables, lean proteins, and whole grains. Stay hydrated and be mindful of your eating habits.

c. Adequate Sleep: Prioritize sufficient and quality sleep. Establish a consistent sleep schedule and create a sleep-conducive environment.

3. Spiritual Health:

a. Reflection and Contemplation: Set aside time for self-reflection and contemplation. This can be through prayer, meditation, or simply spending quiet moments in nature.

b. Connect with Your Beliefs: Engage with your spiritual or philosophical beliefs. Attend religious services, read sacred content, or participate in activities that align with your spiritual values.

c. Community and Support: Surround yourself with a supportive community that shares your spiritual or ethical principles. Building connections with others who understand and respect your beliefs can be enriching.

4. Self-Care Practices:

a. Setting Boundaries: Learn to say no when needed and establish healthy boundaries in your personal and professional life.

b. Regular Check-ins: Take time for regular self-assessment. Ask yourself how you feel emotionally, physically, and spiritually, and adjust your self-care practices accordingly.

c. Learning and Growth: Cultivate a mindset of continuous learning and personal growth. This can involve reading, taking courses, or engaging in activities that challenge and inspire you.

Remember that self-care is an ongoing process, and adapting these practices to your unique needs and circumstances is essential. Regularly reassess your well-being and make adjustments as necessary to ensure a balanced and fulfilling life.

Grandma Vernesta's Words of Wisdom on Self-Care:

"Don't let anyone take advantage of you. Don't look like what you have been through."

Reflect on Your Self-Care Journey:

- What does self-care mean to you? How do you currently practice self-care in your daily life?

- What areas of your life feel neglected right now? How can you address these through self-care?

- How does your body feel today? What physical self-care activities can help you feel better?

- How do your physical, emotional, and mental needs differ? What self-care activities support each of these areas?

- How do you connect with your spirituality or sense of purpose? What practices help you feel spiritually fulfilled?

You Don't Know Yourself Yet

Examine yourselves to see whether you are in the faith; test yourselves. Do you not realize that Christ Jesus is in you- unless, of course, you fail the test?

— (2 CORINTHIANS 13:5 NIV)

My Grandmother always had valuable insights about dating. She focused on matters of the heart when giving advice. She emphasized the importance of patience, understanding, and willingness to comprise in a relationship. In my younger years, she defined the characteristics of a lady. She reminded me to respect my mind, body, and identity. I was never to let a man know when I was on my menstrual cycle, flatulate, or even when I needed to go to the restroom. I had to make sure my clothing was modest, my hair could never be out of place, and I was to be always presentable. Even going to bed, I had to be neatly dressed in pajamas or a nightgown. It makes me chuckle when I think about how much emphasis she put on how we looked going to bed.

In my grandmother's wise counsel, she often emphasized that my younger days were a time of self-discovery and growth, and while I may have felt like I understood what it meant to be in love, I was still in the early stages of understanding myself. Drawing from her wealth of experience, she firmly but gently advised me that I might not have the depth of understanding or insight to grasp long-term relationship needs fully. Her advice was a reminder to approach relationships with patience and an open heart, acknowledging that preferences and priorities evolve over time. She encouraged me to appreciate the journey of self-discovery and not rush into commitments prematurely.

Through her guidance, I learned the importance of building a strong foundation within myself before seeking to intertwine my life with another, recognizing that the path to a fulfilling and lasting romantic relationship is often a gradual and enriching process. I didn't always take this advice and made well-intended decisions that weren't the best. I allowed my emotions and internal butterflies to lead me to find love. I didn't give myself an opportunity to explore options, and I think I may have gotten too serious too soon. I don't regret it. I learned from it, but truthfully, if I had to do it all over again, I would not have been in long-term committed relationships early on in my adolescence.

With her wisdom and grace, my grandmother always emphasized the importance of understanding oneself. She often said, "It is best to understand who you are and cultivate self-awareness. This will help you determine the kind of person you are and who you would want as a partner." Her words resonated deeply with me, especially as I transitioned from adolescence into adulthood, facing the complexities of relationships and personal growth.

As a young person, I often found myself pondering her advice, eager to explore the world and its myriad experiences, and I didn't fully grasp the depth of her counsel. She would patiently explain that due to my youth and limited life experiences, I wasn't able to make sound decisions regarding relationships. "You're still learning, still growing," she would say. "Take this time to understand yourself first."

When I was about to leave for college, her advice became even more poignant. She advised me not to rush into a committed relationship but rather to spend those formative years getting to know myself. "Use this time to develop into the woman God wants you to be and to fulfill your purpose," she urged. It was a directive that shaped my college years and, ultimately, my life.

Entering college, I was eager to embrace independence and the opportunities for growth and self-discovery. My Grandmother's words were a steady compass, guiding me through the excitement and challenges of this new chapter. I was a student-athlete, but outside of that, I engaged in activities that pushed me out of my comfort zone. Each experience contributed to my understanding of who I was and who I wanted to become.

I began to realize that self-awareness was not just about recognizing my strengths and weaknesses but also about understanding my values, passions, and the kind of life I wanted to lead. This introspection allowed me to set boundaries, make informed decisions, and approach relationships with a clear sense of what I wanted and needed.

During my freshman year, I met many people and formed numerous friendships. Some of these friendships blossomed into deeper connections, but I heeded my grandmother's advice and refrained from rushing into romantic relationships. Instead, I focused on building a strong foundation for myself. I journaled regularly, reflecting on my experiences and emotions. This practice of self-reflection was crucial in developing a deeper understanding of my identity and aspirations. Through these interactions, I learned empathy, resilience, and the importance of compassion. These qualities became integral to my character and influenced the kind of partner I aspired to be.

As I navigated through college, I encountered challenges that tested my resolve and self-awareness. My Grandmother's guidance also led me to explore my spiritual beliefs more deeply. I attended various religious and spiritual gatherings, read books on spirituality, and engaged in discussions with peers and mentors. This exploration helped me connect with my faith and understand its role in shaping my values and purpose. It reinforced the idea that personal and spiritual growth are intertwined, each enriching the other.

By the time I graduated, I had a much clearer sense of who I was and what I wanted from life. I had developed a strong sense of self-awareness that allowed me to approach relationships with intention and clarity. I knew that a healthy relationship required two individuals who understood and valued themselves and could support each other's growth and aspirations. Reflecting on my grandmother's advice, I realized that her wisdom went beyond relationships. It was about living a fulfilling and purposeful life.

By understanding myself and aligning my actions with my values, I pursued a career I was passionate about and built meaningful and supportive relationships. Her guidance also taught me the importance of patience and timing. She reminded me that true growth and understanding take time in a world that often encourages us to rush and achieve quickly. By being patient with myself and my journey, I was able to appreciate the process of becoming and not just the end goal. As I moved into adulthood, I carried her wisdom with me. It influenced my approach to career decisions, friendships, and personal development. I continued to prioritize self-awareness, regularly checking in with myself to ensure that my actions and choices were aligned with my values and purpose.

In my romantic relationships, I applied the lessons I had learned. I sought partners who were also self-aware and who valued personal growth. I communicated openly about my goals and aspirations and encouraged my partners to do the same. This approach fostered relationships that were built on mutual respect, understanding, and support.

My Grandmother's advice also taught me the importance of resilience. Life is unpredictable, and there are times when things don't go as planned. By understanding myself and my values, I was able to navigate setbacks with grace and determination. I learned to see challenges as opportunities for growth and to trust that each experience was part of my journey toward becoming the person I was meant to be.

Her wisdom has been a guiding light throughout my life. It has helped me develop a strong sense of self, approach relationships with clarity and intention, and live a life aligned with my values and purpose. As I continue to grow and evolve, I am grateful for her guidance and the foundation it has provided.

My Grandmother's teachings have also inspired me to share her wisdom with others. I mentor young women, encouraging them to take the time to understand themselves and to prioritize their personal growth. I remind them that self-awareness is a powerful tool that can lead to fulfilling relationships and a purposeful life.

**Grandma Vernesta's Words of
Wisdom on Knowing Yourself:**
*"Take time to get to know yourself before
making important decisions."*

Reflect on Your Journey on Self-Awareness:

- What core values guide your life and decisions? How do they influence your current decision-making process?

- What are your long-term goals and aspirations? How does this decision align with or diverge from these goals?

- Are you prioritizing the opinions of others over your own needs or desires? If so, why?

- Is your current mental state conducive to making a well-thought-out decision? Do you need more time or support?

- Who are the key people in your life who can provide support and guidance regarding making decisions?

The Lord Giveth and the Lord Taketh Away

*Naked I came from my mother's womb,
and naked I will depart. The Lord gave,
and the Lord has taken away; may
the name of the Lord be praised.*

– (JOB 1:21 NIV)

It is no surprise that funeralizing six family members took a traumatic toll on any family. In 1966, there were so many obstacles Black families faced. At thirty-eight, my grandmother became a widowed mother of six children due to a fire in the family's home. All their possessions had been destroyed. She was a stay-at-home mother and had to pick up the pieces. Their lives had forever changed.

She was met with other obstacles as she adjusted to her new way of living. Three months after losing her family, her brother was brutally murdered in Baltimore, Maryland. She was the oldest of nine children and was a source of stability and assurance for her siblings. Her siblings were concerned that she wouldn't be able to handle the news, but she

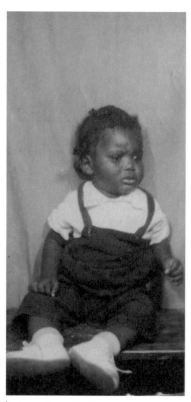

Larry Darnell Lilly at age 9 months old

persisted and assumed her role as the oldest sibling. My Grandmother, now grappling with an unimaginable tragedy, finds herself enveloped in profound and overwhelming grief. Despite the immense tragedy that had befallen her, my grandmother displayed remarkable resilience as she courageously continued to navigate life and raise the remaining members of her family.

Every day was a struggle, marked by the absence of five beloved children and a husband who once shared the joys and challenges of parenthood. Yet, she found strength in the responsibility of caring for those who remain. The family's days were filled with a bittersweet mix of memories and the pressing demands of the present. The void left by the loss of their loved ones echoed through the halls of their home, a constant reminder of the irreplaceable bonds severed by the tragic fire. Amidst all the grief, she persevered, drawing on an inner strength that defied the weight of sorrow.

Parenting the surviving family members became an even more profound endeavor as she strived to provide love, support, and a semblance of normalcy despite the shadows cast by the tragedy. There were moments of joy tinged with sadness, as celebrations and milestones were marked by the presence of cherished family members and friends who knew her story. My Grandmother became a beacon of resilience for her immediate and extended family, imparting valuable lessons in faith, fortitude, and the enduring nature of familial love. Her resilience did not erase the pain, but it allowed her to continue living, embracing the role of a guiding force for our family, ensuring that the legacy of her children and husband lives on through shared memories and the indomitable spirit she brought to each day. She demonstrated the strength needed to support her parents and siblings. She attended the funeral of her oldest brother while grieving her husband and children. She never attributed her strength to her own doing. It was God who continued to sustain her and give her strength.

Sunday, March 6, 1966, was no different from any other Sunday for the Lilly family of thirteen. It was the regular Sunday church service, followed by visiting family members. It wasn't until the arrival home that this Sunday actually turned out to be very different. The two youngest daughters, Shirley Ann and Jo Ann were in the kitchen singing and rocking in their rocking chairs. A few of the older children were in the back discussing the day's event. Not all the children were at home. It was unusual for a school night, but my grandmother decided to allow two of her children to stay the night at her in-laws' house. Their three-month-old baby Alvin was down for his afternoon nap. My Grandfather decided to add more wood to the wood-burning stove. It was then that life would never be the same.

The stove combusted, and the house immediately went into flames. My Grandmother was walking a neighbor out of the house who had just stopped by to see the new baby. My Grandmother turned around to try and go inside, but the house was in flames. The neighbor grabbed her by the arms. The older children who were out back were able to escape. The younger ones were in the kitchen and had already been consumed by the smoke and fire.

My Grandfather, while on fire, ran to try and put himself out of the fire. He was not successful. There were only three people who escaped the fire: my mother, Grandmother, and one uncle. My Grandfather and one uncle were transported to the Chapel Hill burn center. They succumbed to burns and smoke inhalation on March 7 and 8, respectively. In a matter of hours, my 38-year-old Grandmother lost her 46-year-old husband and five children ages twelve, six, three, two, and three months old. How could this happen? Why did this happen? Everything they owned was gone.

There, she stood grounded in her faith and recalled days earlier the Holy Spirit speaking to her, saying, "If you lost everything, what would you do?" In the days leading up to the funeral, she said she told God to take the heaviness of grief away from her and to keep her. The day of the funeral, she went behind her mother's home to spend alone time with God and recalled saying the Lord Giveth and the Lord Taketh away. She arrived at the funeral to be met with a crowd of over 2000 people. As she and her children made their way through the crowd, her brother reached out to grab her but didn't need to. She made her way to her pew. There, she sat with six caskets directly in front of her.

The unimaginable life-altering events could bring someone to a mental breakdown and cause them to give up. Instead, she trusted God and reminded him of his words that he would never leave her or forsake her, and she depended on him. Her message to her children was that they had to keep living. She had six more children to continue raising. She said to them, "It's just us now; we have to stick together as a family." When she spoke of their deaths, she would also talk from a perspective of faith. "Life presents us with challenges that sometimes feel insurmountable. When someone we love dearly is no longer with us, the pain can be overwhelming. It's just us now, and we have to keep living. I know that Mack is gone, and the void left by his absence is profound. But we must find the strength to move forward, even when it feels impossible."

"Mack was an integral part of our lives, and his absence is felt deeply by everyone who knew him. He brought joy, laughter, and love into our lives, and his memory will always be cherished. However, as difficult as it is to say goodbye, we must find a way to continue living our lives. It's just us now, and we have to keep living.

"Grieving is a natural response to loss, and it's okay to cry. In fact, it's necessary. Tears are a way of expressing our sorrow and pain, and they help us process our emotions. Allow yourself to feel the sadness, to miss Mack, and to remember the moments you shared. Hold on to the precious memories and let them bring you comfort. However, while it is important to grieve, it is equally important not to let grief consume us. We cannot stay in that place of sorrow indefinitely.

"When the pain feels too great and the sadness too deep, I want you to turn to God. In times of hurt and longing, seek comfort in your faith. God is always there, ready to provide solace and strength. When you miss Mack, let your prayers be a bridge to the divine, where you can find peace and reassurance. In the quiet moments of prayer and reflection, you can feel God's presence and know that you are not alone.

"Faith is a powerful source of comfort and strength. It can help us navigate difficult times and find hope in the midst of sorrow. When you feel lost and overwhelmed, turn to God. Pray for strength, for peace, and for the ability to carry on. Trust that God is with you, guiding you and supporting you through this journey.

"We will all have to go see the Lord one day. This truth is a part of our human existence. Knowing this, we must cherish the time we have and live our lives fully. We honor those we've lost by continuing to live, love, and find joy in the world around us. Mack's memory will live on in our hearts, and his legacy will be reflected in the way we choose to carry on.

"Joanne, Shirley Ann, Larry, Charles Lewis, Alvin Wayne, and Mack are where we all want to be. They have found peace and eternal rest in the presence of the Lord. As we remember them, we are reminded of our own journey and the importance of living our lives in a way that honors their memory. We must live right so that we can make it to heaven, where we will be reunited with our loved ones.

"Living a righteous life means following the teachings of Jesus. It means loving one another, showing compassion, and striving to do good in the world. It means seeking forgiveness for our mistakes and striving to be better each day. By following Jesus, we can find the strength and guidance we need to live our lives in a way that honors God and prepares us for eternal life.

"In the face of loss, it can be easy to lose sight of our faith and our purpose. But it is in these moments that our faith is most important. It is our faith that gives us hope and helps us find meaning in our suffering. It is our faith that reminds us that we are not alone and that we are loved by a compassionate and merciful God.

"Let's support each other through this journey, leaning on our faith and the strength of our community. We can find hope in the promise of eternal life and the comfort of knowing that one day, we will be reunited with our loved ones in the presence of the Lord. In the meantime, we must keep living. We must embrace the days ahead, finding purpose and meaning in our lives. It's okay to feel sad, and it's okay to cry, but we must also find moments of happiness and reasons to smile. Turn to God for guidance, and let your faith be the light that leads you through the darkness. Together, we will navigate this path, honoring Mack's memory by living our lives to the fullest.

"The memories of Joanne, Shirley Ann, Larry, Charles Lewis, Alvin Wayne, and Mack should inspire us to live better lives. They have shown us what living with love, kindness, and integrity means. We must carry forward their legacy by embodying these values in our own lives. Each day is an opportunity to make choices that reflect our faith and our commitment to living a righteous life.

"Life is a precious gift, and we must not take it for granted. Even in the midst of sorrow, there is beauty and joy to be found. We must open our hearts to the blessings that each day brings and find gratitude in the small moments of happiness. It is through this gratitude that we can find the strength to carry on and to live our lives with purpose.

"As we move forward, let us remember that we are not alone. We have each other, and we have our faith. Together, we can support one another, find strength in our community, and draw comfort from our shared beliefs. Let us be there for each other, offering a listening ear, a comforting hug, and words of encouragement.

"In times of difficulty, reflecting on the lessons our loved ones have taught us can be helpful. What would Mack say to us now? How would he want us to live our lives? I believe he would want us to find joy, to love deeply, and to live our lives with integrity. He would want us to cherish our memories of him and carry forward his spirit in our actions and hearts.

"We can also find comfort in the rituals and traditions of our faith. Attending church, reading scripture, and praying can provide a sense of connection to God and our community. These practices can help us find peace and strength in the midst of our grief. They remind us of the eternal nature of God's love and our hope in the promise of eternal life.

"As we continue to navigate this journey, let us also remember to take care of ourselves. Grief can be physically and emotionally exhausting, and finding ways to nurture our well-being is important. This might include finding time for rest, engaging in activities that bring us joy, and seeking support from friends, family, or a counselor. Taking care of ourselves allows us to be better able to support those around us and to live our lives more fully.

"In the quiet moments of reflection, let us also take time to listen to our own hearts. What are our hopes and dreams? What are the ways that we can honor the memory of our loved ones in our own lives? By tuning into our own inner voice, we can find guidance and direction for the path ahead.

"As we move forward, let us do so with a sense of purpose and determination. Let us commit to living our lives in a way that honors the memory of those we have lost. Let us find ways to positively impact the world, spread love and kindness, and live our lives with integrity and faith.

"Mack, Joanne, Shirley Ann, Larry, Charles Lewis, and Alvin Wayne may no longer be with us in body, but their spirit lives on in our hearts. Their legacy is a part of us, and we carry it forward in the way we live our lives. By living with love, kindness, and faith, we honor their memory and ensure that their spirit continues to touch the world.

"In the end, it is our faith that sustains us. Our faith gives us hope and helps us find meaning in the midst of sorrow. It is our faith that reminds us that we are loved by a compassionate and merciful God. Let us hold on to that faith and let it guide us through the days ahead.

"As we continue to navigate this journey, let us do so with a sense of hope and determination. Let us find ways to honor the memory of our loved ones, to live our lives with purpose and integrity, and to support one another with love and compassion. It is just us now, but we are not alone. We have each other, and we have our faith. And with that, we can find the strength to keep living.

"In the days, weeks, and months ahead, let us take comfort in the knowledge that our loved ones are at peace in the presence of the Lord. They have found eternal rest, and one day, we will be reunited with them in heaven. Until that day comes, let us live our lives in a way that honors their memory and reflects our faith. Let us find strength in our community, comfort in our faith, and hope in the promise of eternal life.

"Together, we can navigate this journey, finding meaning and purpose in our lives and honoring the memory of those we have lost. It is just us now, but we have the strength and the faith to keep living. And with God's guidance, we can find the courage to move forward, one step at a time."

Grandma Vernesta's Words of Wisdom on Grief:
"We all belong to God. This earthly home is temporary."

Reflect on Your Grief Journey:

- How does the belief that "the Lord giveth and the Lord taketh away" help you in accepting the loss of a loved one? Reflect on how this understanding can bring you peace and acceptance in your grief journey.

- In what ways can you find gratitude for the time you had with your loved one, recognizing them as a gift from the Lord? List specific memories or qualities you are thankful for and how they have enriched your life.

- How can the concept that everything is within God's plan help you find meaning in your loss? Reflect on how your faith can guide you in seeking purpose and understanding in the midst of grief.

- How can you strengthen your trust in God's plan for your life, even when faced with the pain of loss? Write about ways you can lean on your faith and find comfort in knowing that God is in control.

- How does your faith in the Lord's ultimate wisdom and love provide hope for the future? Reflect on the ways this belief can help you move forward, finding hope and strength in the promise of eternal life and eventual reunion with your loved ones.

It's Not How Much Money You Make, It's How You Spend It That Matters

Why spend money on what is not bread, and your labor on what does not satisfy?
Listen, listen to me, and eat what is good, and you will delight in the richest of fare.

— (ISAIAH 55:2 NIV)

Being a housewife and mother of eleven children was my grandmother's primary occupation. Losing her spouse, who was the breadwinner and provider, created a necessity to seek employment. She never had to work outside the home until the pivotal moment of losing her husband. During their marriage, he was the consummate provider. The amount of security and psychological safety he provided her with was unmatched. Having a supportive spouse who knows your needs before you know your own is the epitome of being equally yoked. Now that my grandfather, the breadwinner, was gone, she had to find work to provide for the family.

There were odds and ends jobs such as babysitting, cleaning homes, and being a caretaker of children in their own homes. The pay was often not enough to make ends meet. She had always been a good financial steward. Yet, this was a different set of circumstances. She was left now to manage the household. Outside of caring for the children, she had not managed the financial responsibilities of the home. There was little to no contact with the mortgage company or any of the business owners my grandfather had a relationship with. Yet, she knew it had to be done.

Grandma Vernesta with Granddaughter Crystal and Great Grand children Miles and Morgan

Her focus was to limit any disruption in the lives of her children. The jobs she was working on were inconsistent and based on the needs of the employer. There were also the post-funeral affairs that needed to be taken care of. My grandfather left quite a bit of land and other assets for her to manage. She also had no home because it had been lost in the fire. My Grandmother's mother offered her and her children to live with them until she could get on her feet. She declined.

Instead, she wanted to ensure she had a home for her children. She rented a home across the street from her mother. All the children were school-aged, so she could work outside the home. She was now responsible for paying the bills and ensuring there was a home to maintain. My grandfather taught her a number of business lessons about managing her finances and dealing with business owners. She used the insurance money to build a new house on the same land that was once occupied by the home that caught fire. The house fire occurred in March 1966. She moved into her home in the summer of 1968. She continued to live there for thirty-two years until she bought another home when the city wanted to purchase the land for commercial use.

I learned the value of a dollar from her. For my first job, I made $5.25 an hour. I worked for a popular fast-food chain, and watching my grandmother be conscientious with her money showed me that it wasn't the amount of money you make; it's what you do with it. She sought employment as a housekeeper at the local hospital. She worked in housekeeping for nearly twenty years. Her compensation was never more than $6.48 an hour, but she was able to build a quality lifestyle on that salary. Working at a job that paid $6.48 an hour, she knew that every penny counted. It was a struggle to make ends meet, but she never let her circumstances define her. Instead, she embraced the principles of good stewardship and faithful tithing, believing wholeheartedly in the promise that God blesses those who are faithful with a few things.

She managed her money with remarkable discipline and wisdom. Each paycheck was carefully budgeted, ensuring that her essential needs were met first. She understood the importance of living within her means and prioritized saving wherever she could. Her meticulous approach to finances meant that she rarely indulged in unnecessary luxuries, yet she always found ways to make her money stretch further.

A significant part of her financial discipline was her commitment to tithing. Despite her modest income, she faithfully set aside 10% of her earnings for the church. This act of giving was not just a religious obligation for her; it was a tangible expression of her faith and trust in God's provision. She believed in the biblical principle that giving back to God a portion of what He had given her would open the doors to greater blessings. Her tithing was an act of worship and a testament to her belief that God would honor her faithfulness.

God saw how faithful she was with a few things and blessed her abundantly. Over time, her diligence and faith bore fruit. Her careful management of money, combined with her unwavering faith, led to unexpected opportunities and blessings. She received promotions and better job offers, gradually increasing her income, but still, she only reached $6.48

an hour. Her financial wisdom grew alongside her earnings, allowing her to save more and invest wisely.

With time, her savings grew substantial. She made smart investments and continued to live frugally, ensuring her newfound wealth was managed with the same care as her initial earnings. Her commitment to good stewardship never wavered. She used her resources wisely, always mindful of the lessons she had learned during her leaner years.

Her discipline and faithfulness enabled her to achieve what once seemed impossible. She built not just one but two homes. Each home was a testament to her hard work, careful planning, and God's blessings. They stood as symbols of her journey from modest beginnings to a life of prosperity. These homes were not just physical structures; they represented security, stability, and the fulfillment of her dreams.

Living a fruitful life, she never forgot the importance of giving. Her generosity extended beyond tithing to the church. She supported charitable causes, helped those in need, and always sought ways to give back to her community. Her life was a living example of the biblical principle that it is more blessed to give than to receive. Her generosity inspired those around her and demonstrated the power of faithful stewardship.

She knew how to manage her money well, a skill evident in every aspect of her life. She dressed well, always presenting herself with dignity and grace. Her wardrobe was a reflection of her understanding that quality often trumps quantity. She invested in timeless, well-made pieces that lasted for years rather than succumbing to fleeting fashion trends. This approach saved her money in the long run and ensured that she always looked polished and put together.

Her financial acumen extended to maintaining a hefty savings account. These savings were a source of security and peace of mind, allowing her to navigate life's uncertainties with confidence. She understood the importance of having a financial cushion, and she worked diligently to build and maintain it. These savings were not just a rainy-day fund but a testament to her foresight and discipline.

Her journey from earning $6.48 an hour to living a life of abundance was marked by a deep and abiding faith in God. She believed that her financial success was not just the result of her own efforts but also a reflection of God's faithfulness. She often shared her story with others, using her experiences to encourage and inspire. She emphasized the importance of trusting in God, practicing good stewardship, and being faithful to what one has, no matter how little it may seem.

She also understood that true wealth is not measured solely by material possessions. Her life was rich in relationships, experiences, and the joy of giving. She cultivated deep and meaningful connections with family and friends, always prioritizing people over things. Her homes were places of hospitality and warmth, where she welcomed others and shared the blessings she had received.

In her later years, she reflected on her journey with gratitude and humility. She knew that her story was one of grace and faithfulness, a testament to what can be achieved when one trusts in God and manages one's resources wisely. She continued to live by the principles that had guided her from the beginning, always mindful of the importance of good stewardship and generous giving.

Her life served as a powerful reminder that it is not the amount of money one has that determines one's success but how one manages and uses what they have been given. She taught those around her that it is possible to overcome humble beginnings and achieve great things with faith, discipline, and a generous heart. Her legacy was not just in the homes she built or the savings she accumulated but in the lives she touched and the example she set.

Her story reminds us of the profound wisdom that accompanies good stewardship and faithful tithing. We see the truth of the biblical principle that those who are faithful with a few things will be entrusted with much. Her life is a testament to the power of faith, hard work, and wise management of resources. It is an inspiration to all who seek to live a life of purpose, generosity, and abundance.

In conclusion, her journey from making $6.48 an hour to living a fruitful and prosperous life is a powerful example of the transformative power of faith and good stewardship. Through careful management of her resources, unwavering commitment to tithing, and deep trust in God, she was able to achieve financial stability and live a life of abundance.

Grandma Vernesta's Words of Wisdom on Money:
"It doesn't matter the amount of money you make; it's what you do with it that is important. Always find a way to pay your tithes; God will multiply."

Reflect on Your Money Management Journey:

- How do you currently manage your budget and track your spending? Reflect on your methods for keeping track of income and expenses. What changes can you make to improve your budgeting habits and ensure that your spending aligns with your financial goals?

- How much do you prioritize saving money, and what strategies do you use to save consistently? Consider the importance of having an emergency fund and the steps you can take to build or maintain it. How can you increase your savings rate, even if it's by a small amount each month?

- What is your current approach to managing debt? Reflect on your strategies for paying off debt and preventing new debt from accumulating. What actions can you take to reduce your debt more effectively and avoid common pitfalls?

- How do you plan for your financial future, including retirement and other long-term goals? Consider your current investments and financial planning strategies. What steps can you take to educate yourself about investing and ensure you are making informed decisions that will benefit you in the long run?

- How do your attitudes and beliefs about money influence your financial decisions? Reflect on any limiting beliefs or habits that might be holding you back from achieving financial success. What specific financial goals do you want to set for yourself, and what actionable steps can you take to work towards those goals, regardless of your current income?

Live Your Life and Do What Makes You Happy

Taste and see that the Lord is good; blessed is the one who takes refuge in him.

— (PSALM 34:8 NIV)

Do what makes you feel good on the inside. One of my favorite pastimes was late-evening desserts with my grandmother. She had a sweet tooth and always seemed to want to have dessert of some sort on hand. There was something sweet in the house, whether it be a Mr. Goodbar, her all-time favorite candy bar, vanilla ice cream, cookies, or a piece of homemade cake she would have frozen from a previous holiday.

She would often take a nap around 3:00 pm, and after dinner, and into the evening, around 6:30 pm, she would ask if I wanted something sweet. I usually didn't, but I would say yes. She would then tell me what she wanted. I would oblige. She would get up from her nap and walk into the kitchen.

I would prepare the dessert and have it waiting for her. We always ate the same thing. If she wanted a piece of pound cake and vanilla ice cream, that's what we both had. It became a conversation piece. As we ate, she would ask, "Doesn't this taste so good?" I would reply, "Yes, ma'am. It sure does." She would smile and continue the conversation with a life story.

These dessert moments occurred frequently throughout the week. It became a ritual of some sort with her. I would often look up from my ice cream, or whatever the choice of dessert was, and watch her eat. She seemed to savor every bite and made what she was eating look so delicious. Although we had the same dessert, I wanted to taste hers. I thought surely hers tasted better than mine.

She would eat slowly and talk to me with such intention. She would say things like, "Crys, always remember to keep God first. When you do that, you know that everything will be alright." I used to wonder, what in the world could go wrong? I didn't ask many questions. I would mostly listen. I would ask, "Grandma, are things going to go wrong?" She would reply, "Baby if you live long enough, you will see and experience some things, and trouble will come, but if you are living right and trust God, everything will be alright." She would continue to eat her ice cream, smile to reassure me, and continue with her story.

I looked forward to having dessert in the evenings, but mostly, I looked forward to hearing the stories about life and how I should conduct myself in all situations. After experiencing life and some of the troubles that my grandmother mentioned would come, I now realize what those dessert moments in the kitchen were for. She took her time enjoying the things that she loved. My Grandmother was diagnosed with diabetes later on, but she still found a way to enjoy those desserts and would say, "I only took a pinch. I didn't eat much, and it was so good!"

She invested her time in me in those moments by sharing one of her favorite things: desserts. She always kept the items she loved on hand so that she could enjoy what she loved to do and satisfy her love for sweets at any given moment. It was not an expensive ordeal or gesture to find quality time with me. I'm confident that she knew her pouring into me would benefit me for years to come.

Create a space for the things you love and the people you love. Bring the people you love along to stop and enjoy the little things in life that matter. Whatever makes your soul happy, do it. My Grandmother was a firm believer in this principle, and she lived her life with an infectious joy that taught me the importance of pursuing what truly brings happiness and fulfillment. One of her simple pleasures was indulging in sweets, particularly vanilla ice cream and cookies, as an evening snack. Her eyes would light up as she enjoyed these treats, and she often shared them with us, making these moments even more special.

My Grandmother's love for vanilla ice cream and cookies was more than just a preference for certain foods; it was a reflection of her philosophy on life. She believed that life is too short to deny oneself the simple joys that make the soul happy. She often said, "Do what makes your soul happy and do it with no regrets. Ignore what others might say." This mantra was a guiding principle in her life and has deeply influenced how I live mine.

I observed my grandmother embrace the things that brought her joy without hesitation or guilt. Whether it was her evening snack of ice cream and cookies, tending to her garden, or spending time with her loved ones, she did it all with a sense of purpose and delight. She taught me that true happiness comes from within and that it's important to honor what brings us joy, regardless of external opinions or societal pressures.

There were times when others would question or criticize her choices. Some people would comment on her indulgence in sweets, suggesting that it wasn't the healthiest option for someone her age. Others would raise eyebrows at her passionate dedication to her hobbies, wondering why she invested so much time and energy into activities that didn't seem particularly productive. But my grandmother never let these comments deter her. She understood that happiness is a deeply personal experience and that only she could determine what truly brought her joy.

Her wisdom has stayed with me, serving as a constant reminder to prioritize my own happiness. In a world where we are often bombarded with messages about what we should or shouldn't do to be happy, it can be easy to lose sight of what truly matters to us. My Grandmother's example has taught me to listen to my inner voice and to pursue the things that make my soul happy, regardless of external opinions.

For me, this means carving out time for activities that bring me joy, even if they seem insignificant or frivolous to others. Whether it's reading a good book, going for a long walk in nature, indulging in my favorite dessert, or spending time with loved ones, I make a conscious effort to prioritize these moments. I have learned that when I honor my own happiness, I am better able to bring joy and positivity to those around me.

Of course, there are times when pursuing what makes us happy requires courage and resilience. We may face criticism, doubt, or even outright opposition from others. In these moments, I draw strength from my grandmother's example. She showed me that it's possible to stand firm in our choices and to pursue our happiness with confidence and grace. Her unwavering commitment to her own joy has given me the courage to do the same, even in the face of adversity.

One particular memory stands out to me. It was a summer evening, and we were sitting on the porch, enjoying our usual treat of vanilla ice cream and cookies. I was going through a difficult time, feeling torn between following my own path and meeting the expectations of others. My Grandmother must have sensed my inner turmoil, for she turned to me with a knowing smile and said, "Life is full of choices, and not all of them will be easy. But remember, whatever makes your soul happy, do it. You'll never regret being true to yourself."

Her words resonated deeply with me, and they continue to guide me to this day. They remind me that true happiness comes from living authentically and honoring our own needs and desires. They encourage me to make choices that align with my values and passions, even when it means going against the grain.

As I navigate the ups and downs of life, I strive to keep my grandmother's wisdom at the forefront of my mind. I remind myself that it's okay to prioritize my own happiness and to pursue the things that bring me joy. This doesn't mean that I ignore the needs of others or shirk my responsibilities, but rather that I find a balance between caring for myself and those around me.

In my relationships, I have found that when I am happy and fulfilled, I am better able to support and uplift others. By being true to myself and pursuing my happiness, I can bring more positivity and joy to my interactions with others. I have learned that when we honor our own needs, we are better equipped to be present and compassionate for those we care about.

Moreover, my grandmother's approach to life has taught me the importance of savoring the small moments of joy. Life is made up of countless little moments, and it's in these moments that true happiness can be found. Whether it's enjoying a favorite treat, spending time with loved ones, or simply taking a moment to appreciate the beauty of nature, these small joys add up to a life well-lived.

In conclusion, whatever makes your soul happy, do it. My Grandmother's love for sweets, particularly vanilla ice cream and cookies, was a simple yet profound expression of her belief in the importance of pursuing what brings us joy. Her wisdom has taught me to prioritize my own happiness and to pursue it without regrets. By ignoring external opinions and focusing on what truly matters to us, we can live a more authentic and fulfilling life.

My Grandmother's example has shown me that true happiness comes from within and that it's important to honor our own needs and desires. Whether it's through small daily joys or larger life choices, we have the power to create a life that aligns with our passions and values. By doing what makes our souls happy, we enrich our lives and bring more positivity and joy to those around us.

As I continue my journey, I carry my grandmother's wisdom with me, reminding myself to embrace the things that bring me joy and live my life with no regrets. Her legacy of happiness and authenticity serves as a guiding light, inspiring me to pursue my own path with confidence and grace. Whatever makes your soul happy, do it. This simple yet profound principle has the power to transform our lives and the lives of those around us, creating a ripple effect of joy and fulfillment.

Grandma Vernesta's Words of Wisdom on Enjoying Life:
"Do what makes you happy. You have your own life to live.

Reflect on Your Journey:

➤ What activities or hobbies bring you the most joy and fulfillment? Reflect on the things you love to do and why they make you happy. How can you incorporate more of these activities into your daily or weekly routine?

➤ What are you truly passionate about? Think about the subjects, causes, or interests that excite and motivate you. How can you dedicate more time and energy to pursuing your passions and integrating them into your life?

➤ How do you balance your responsibilities with leisure and relaxation? Reflect on your current work-life balance and identify areas where you can make adjustments. What steps can you take to ensure that you have enough time to relax and enjoy life outside of your obligations?

➤ What small, everyday moments bring you happiness? Consider the little things that brighten your day, such as enjoying a cup of coffee in the morning, spending time in nature, or connecting with loved ones. How can you be more mindful of these moments and create opportunities for happiness throughout your day?

➤ What specific goals can you set to increase your overall happiness and well-being? Reflect on areas of your life where you would like to experience more joy and satisfaction. What actionable steps can you take to achieve these goals and create a life that truly makes you happy?

CHAPTER 10

Seldom Visits Make Longtime Friends

*Seldom set foot in your neighbor's house—
too much of you, and they will hate you.*

— (PROVERBS 25:17 NIV)

I never witnessed my grandmother entertain cliques or have multiple people in and out of her house. She was never one who had to have a crowd around her. There weren't many people who would visit her. There were phone calls from friends. However, there were never frequent visits. These friends were known to us. They would call, and we knew them by voice, not just by name. Though we didn't always see them, we knew they were close to her. They were her tribe.

This handful of women had been around since before I was born, and the same women were around through my adulthood. We didn't always see them, but her sisters in Christ, Sisters Vivian, Ms. Ethel, Sister Evelyn, Ms. Gwen, and Cousin Elma were constant callers. They had a profound impact on our entire family. We all knew who they were because the quality of their friendship stood the test of time. As long as I can remember, they were a part of our lives.

My Grandmother's friendships taught me something. Friendships can transcend the limitations of sporadic visits or infrequent phone calls. In today's fast-paced world, where distance and busyness often impact and separate the closest of friends, genuine friendships will endure throughout time.

I learned that genuine friendships are built on trust, mutual respect, and unwavering support. All priceless and intangible. I learned that genuine friendships provide a sense of companionship and emotional security. In my darkest of times, I knew who I could rely on. Often plagued by a vast amount of distrust because I had been disappointed, I called to my remembrance how there were the faithful who stood alongside me, cried, fought, and held me up. It was the friends who lived seven hours away, who had been there through ups and downs, offering me encouragement, honesty, and a profound connection that was not superficial.

In today's fast-paced world, the concept of friendship has evolved. Gone are the days when friendships were solely measured by the frequency of interactions or daily communications. Instead, the emphasis has shifted towards the depth and quality of the bond shared. The idea that "seldom visits make long-time friends" underscores the essence of true friendship: it is not the quantity of time spent together that defines the strength of a friendship, but the quality of understanding, support, and unconditional love that persists, regardless of physical distance or infrequent contact.

Friendships that endure the test of time are built on a foundation of mutual respect and deep emotional connection. These relationships are often characterized by an intrinsic understanding of each other's thoughts and feelings, even without the need for constant verbal communication. Friends who have known each other for a long time develop a unique rapport that allows them to pick up right where they left off, no matter how much time has passed since their last interaction. This phenomenon is a testament to the enduring nature of their bond.

One of the key reasons why seldom visits can strengthen long-term friendships is the concept of "space." Giving each other space to grow and pursue individual interests is crucial in any relationship. Space allows individuals to develop their own identities, achieve personal goals, and gather new experiences. When friends come back together after some time apart, they bring fresh perspectives and stories to share, enriching the friendship. This space also prevents the relationship from becoming stagnant or monotonous, as there is always something new to discuss and explore.

Moreover, time apart can help the heart grow fonder. When friends are not constantly in each other's presence, they have the opportunity to miss each other. This longing can reinforce the appreciation and value they place on the friendship. In this context, absence truly makes the heart grow fonder, as the anticipation of reuniting can strengthen the emotional bond between friends. It serves as a reminder of the importance and irreplaceability of the friendship.

The quality of a friendship is often evident in the level of support and unconditional love that friends provide to each other. True friends are those who stand by each other during difficult times, offering a shoulder to lean on and words of encouragement. They celebrate each other's successes and provide comfort during failures. This unwavering support does not require daily communication; it is a constant, underlying presence that can be called upon whenever needed.

Unconditional love is another hallmark of a quality friendship. It is a type of love that is free from judgment and conditions. Friends who love each other unconditionally accept each other's flaws and imperfections. They do not impose unrealistic expectations or demand constant validation. Instead, they offer a safe space where both can be their authentic selves. This type of love fosters a deep sense of trust and security within the friendship.

Furthermore, the understanding that comes with long-term friendships is invaluable. Friends who have known each other for a long time often develop an intuitive understanding of each other's needs and emotions. They can sense when something is wrong, even if nothing is said. This understanding allows them to offer support in the most appropriate and meaningful ways. It is a level of empathy that is cultivated over years of shared experiences and mutual respect.

In addition to emotional support, long-term friendships often involve a shared history that cannot be replicated. Friends who have known each other for many years have a wealth of memories and experiences that form a unique bond. These shared experiences create a sense of continuity and belonging. They serve as a reminder of the journey that the friends have been on together and the growth they have witnessed in each other.

It is also important to recognize that friendships, like any other relationship, require effort and commitment. While seldom visits can strengthen a friendship, it is crucial to maintain a level of communication that works for both parties. This does not necessarily mean frequent

Charles Lewis Lilly age 9

interactions but rather meaningful and intentional communication when it does occur. It could be a phone call, a text message, or even a handwritten letter. The key is to stay connected in a way that reinforces the bond and shows that the friendship is valued.

Grandma Vernesta's Words of Wisdom on Friendship:
"Limit the time you spend in other people's homes.
Make your house a home to enjoy and stay in it."

Reflect on Your Friendship Journey:

- Think about a specific memory or experience you shared with your long-time friend that holds significant meaning to you. How did this experience shape your friendship? Reflect on the importance of these shared moments and how they contribute to the bond you share.

- How do you currently stay in touch with your long-time friend when visits are infrequent? Reflect on the methods you use to maintain your connection, such as phone calls, video chats, or social media. What can you do to enhance these interactions and keep the bond strong despite the distance?

- When was the last time you visited your long-time friend, and what made it memorable? Reflect on the positive aspects of that visit and think about how you can plan future visits to create new memories. What steps can you take to make these visits more frequent or meaningful?

- How do you express your appreciation and gratitude for your long-time friend? Reflect on the qualities you admire in them and the ways they have positively impacted on your life. Consider writing a letter or message to express your feelings and let them know how much they mean to you.

- How have life changes, such as career moves, family commitments, or personal growth, affected your friendship over the years? Reflect on how both of you have adapted to these changes and continued to support each other. What can you do to ensure that your friendship remains strong and evolves positively with time?

Be Sweet, Your Attitude and Personality Mean Everything

Gracious words are a honeycomb, sweet to the soul and healing to the bones.

– (PROVERBS 16:24 NIV)

Always be sweet no matter what. Show people how to behave. Feed them with loving, kind, and gentle words and actions. Don't let how they've treated you impact how you treat them.

My Grandmother embodied these principles, and through her, I learned the profound impact of kindness and respect. She taught me lessons that have shaped my understanding of human interaction and the importance of treating others with unwavering respect and compassion.

In her senior years, I often took my grandmother to the store. Despite her age, she maintained a humble and dignified demeanor. Whenever she interacted with the younger store associates, she always addressed them with "yes ma'am" and "no ma'am." As a young person, this baffled me. I used to get so frustrated with her and tell her she didn't have to do that because they were younger. However, her response was always gentle but firm. She would say, "Baby, I want to show them they are respected for helping me. We don't know how that might make them feel."

At the time, I didn't fully understand the significance of her words. To me, it seemed unnecessary to show such deference to people younger than her. Yet, as I watched her, I began to see the magic in her approach. Her politeness was not just a formality but an intentional act of kindness. She understood that everyone, regardless of age or position, deserves to feel valued and respected. By treating the store associates with such courtesy, she was acknowledging their efforts and contributions, however small they might seem.

Moreover, my grandmother was always intentional about smiling at those she encountered. Her smile was warm, inviting, and genuine. It was a small gesture, but it had a significant impact. People responded to her smiles with their own, and I could see how it brightened their day, even if just momentarily. It was through these simple acts that she spread kindness and positivity wherever she went.

These experiences with my grandmother taught me that respect and kindness are universal languages. They transcend age, background, and circumstance. By being consistently kind and respectful, we have the power to create a ripple effect, influencing others to act similarly. It's a way of showing people how to behave—not through lectures or admonitions but through our actions and attitudes.

There was an incident at the store that remains vivid in my memory. One day, we encountered a young store clerk who seemed particularly stressed. She was juggling multiple tasks, and it was clear she was having a tough day. My Grandmother noticed this immediately. When it was our turn at the checkout, instead of just going through the motions, she took a moment to speak to the clerk. She said, "Thank you for your hard work. I know it must be tough, but you're doing a great job." The clerk's face lit up. She visibly relaxed and managed to smile. It was a small moment, but it highlighted the power of kind words and recognition.

My Grandmother's approach to life taught me a critical lesson: our actions and words matter. They can uplift, encourage, and inspire. Conversely, they can also hurt, demean, and discourage. We have a choice in every interaction, and choosing kindness and respect can make a significant difference in someone's life.

The lessons from my grandmother have stayed with me. In my own life, I strive to follow her example. When dealing with others, whether it's colleagues, strangers, or friends, I try to remember the importance of showing respect and kindness. It's not always easy, especially when others are rude or dismissive. However, I remind myself that I can't control their behavior; I only control my own. Responding with kindness, even in the face of negativity, can sometimes defuse tension and foster a more positive interaction.

In today's fast-paced world, it's easy to overlook the impact of small acts of kindness. We are often so caught up in our own lives and problems that we forget that everyone around us is also fighting their own battles. A smile, a kind word, a gesture of respect—these are small things that require little effort but can have a profound impact. They can make someone's day a little brighter and their burden a little lighter.

Another lesson I learned from my grandmother is the importance of being intentional with our kindness. It's not just about random acts; it's about consistently choosing to act with love and respect. It's about making a conscious effort to see the good in others and to acknowledge it. This kind of intentional kindness can create a culture of respect and compassion in our communities.

My Grandmother also volunteered at a local community center in her senior years. She helped organize events and provided support to those in need. Her involvement was another way she demonstrated her commitment to kindness and respect. She believed in giving back to the community and helping the less fortunate. Through her actions, she showed me that true kindness is about more than just words; it's about taking action to make a positive difference in the world.

Volunteering with her at the community center was an eye-opening experience for me. It gave me a firsthand look at the challenges many people face and the difference that a supportive community can make. My Grandmother treated everyone she met with the same respect and kindness, regardless of their circumstances. She listened to their stories, offered words of encouragement, and provided practical support whenever she could.

One memorable instance was when we were helping to organize a holiday meal for those in need. My Grandmother went out of her way to ensure that the event was special. She believed that everyone deserved to feel valued and cared for, especially during the holidays. Her attention to detail and her genuine care for the guests were evident in everything she did. It was a powerful reminder that even small gestures of kindness can have a lasting impact.

These experiences with my grandmother have profoundly influenced my approach to life. They have taught me that kindness and respect are not just nice-to-have qualities but are essential for creating a better world. They have shown me that we all have the power to make a difference, no matter how small our actions may seem.

In my professional life, I strive to embody these principles. I make it a point to treat my colleagues with respect and kindness, even in challenging situations. I believe that fostering a positive and respectful work environment can lead to better collaboration, increased morale, and ultimately, greater success. When people feel valued and respected, they are more likely to be motivated and engaged in their work.

In my personal life, I try to be a source of positivity and support for those around me. Whether it's through lending a listening ear, offering words of encouragement, or simply being there for someone in need, I aim to make a positive impact. I have found that these acts of kindness not only benefit others but also bring a sense of fulfillment and happiness to my own life.

The lessons from my grandmother continue to guide me every day. They remind me that kindness and respect are powerful tools for creating a better world. They inspire me to be a better person and to strive for a life filled with love, compassion, and respect for others.

Always be sweet no matter what; your attitude and personality mean everything. Show people how to behave by feeding them with loving, kind, and gentle words and actions. Don't let how they've treated you impact how you treat them. These principles, exemplified by my grandmother, have shown me the profound impact that kindness and respect can have on others.

Grandma Vernesta's Words of Wisdom about Being Sweet:
"Your attitude and Personality mean everything.
Always be kind, gracious, and tenderhearted with
your words and actions to everyone you meet."

Reflect on Your Journey:

- Reflect on a recent act of kindness you performed or received. How did it make you feel, and what was the impact on the other person involved? What small, sweet actions can you incorporate into your daily routine to spread kindness to those around you?

- Think about the people you interact with regularly, such as family, friends, coworkers, or strangers. How can you be more attentive to their needs and recognize opportunities to be sweet and supportive? List some specific actions you can take to show kindness in these relationships.

- How often do you give genuine compliments or speak kind words to others? Reflect on the power of positive language and how it can uplift someone's day. What thoughtful compliments or encouraging words can you share with those around you to brighten their spirits?

- Consider a time when you had a disagreement or misunderstanding with someone. How could practicing empathy and showing sweetness have changed the outcome? Reflect on ways you can approach conflicts with more kindness and understanding in the future.

- Think about a random act of sweetness you can perform for someone, whether it's a loved one or a stranger. How can these unexpected gestures make a difference in someone's day? Plan and commit to doing at least one random act of kindness this week and reflect on the experience afterward.

Now and Then, You Have to Do What Must Be Done

Put your outdoor work in order and get your fields ready; after that, build your house.

– (PROVERBS 24:27 NIV)

It became very evident to me at an early age that people often make choices based on their circumstances and personal motivations. In life, we find ourselves in situations where we must make difficult decisions or take necessary actions. My Grandmother knew how to drive but never got her license. My Grandfather attempted to teach her, but she just didn't have a desire to get her license.

Everyone deals with grief differently; for some reason, I think that never getting her license was her way of grieving. It was something that she and my grandfather shared. He took time with her and was very patient with her. As a result of that, my grandmother had to rely on other people to drive her around. It seemingly became a rite of passage and honor to drive her to run errands, to work, or to church. She would always offer gas money. Ma didn't take for granted that she depended on someone else to drive her around.

I recall one time she was waiting for a ride, and the time she had to leave the house so she could be on time was fast approaching. She had to be at work by 6:30 am. She left the house, began walking to work, and hitched a ride with two strangers. She said she prayed all the way there that they wouldn't kill her. They dropped her off at the front of Cape Fear Valley Hospital. It was mostly my mother who took on this responsibility until I got my license. The fact that my grandmother never learned how to drive might seem trivial to some, but in our family, it highlighted a remarkable dynamic of love, resilience, and mutual support. My mother became her primary driver, a role she took on with unwavering commitment and care. Their relationship was a testament to the strength of family bonds and the sacrifices made out of love.

Born in an era when driving wasn't as common for women, especially those juggling multiple roles at home and work, she never embraced driving as a priority. Despite this, she was fiercely independent and resourceful. If she didn't have a ride, which was rare thanks to my mother's dedication, she would start walking. She knew she had to get to work, and she did what she had to do.

My Grandmother's daily routine was a powerful example of her determination. She worked tirelessly to provide for her family and ensure everything ran smoothly. On the rare occasions when my mother couldn't drive her, she would set off on foot without complaint. She viewed each step not as a burden but as a testament to her resilience and commitment. This attitude of doing whatever was necessary left a lasting impression on all of us.

My mother's role as her driver was more than just a task; it was an expression of deep love and respect. My mother juggled her responsibilities, always ensuring that my grandmother got where she needed to be. This arrangement fostered a profound bond between them, built on mutual respect and appreciation. My Grandmother was always so appreciative of my mother's commitment to her. She never took it for granted and often expressed her gratitude through kind words and gestures.

Reflecting on their relationship, I am reminded of the many lessons I've learned from observing them. One of the most significant lessons is the importance of family support. My mother's dedication to my grandmother was unwavering, and in return, my grandmother showed immense gratitude and love. This mutual respect and support created a strong foundation for our family.

**Grandma Vernesta's Words of
Wisdom about Getting Things Done:**
*"Sometimes You Have to Do what you
have to do until you can do better."*

Reflect on Your Journey for Getting Things Done:

- What are the driving forces behind your determination to get things done? How do these motivations influence your actions and decisions? Write about a specific instance where your motivation helped you overcome a significant obstacle.

- Think about a time when you faced a significant challenge while trying to accomplish a goal. How did you navigate this challenge, and what strategies or resources did you use? Reflect on what you learned from this experience and how it shapes your approach to future challenges.

- Describe a moment when you felt like giving up on a task but decided to persevere. What kept you going, and what was the outcome? Reflect on how this experience has influenced your understanding of resilience and the importance of persistence.

- Write about a time when you had to balance multiple priorities to get things done. How did you manage your time and resources? Reflect on what worked well and what could have been improved in your approach.

- Consider how your mindset and attitude affected your ability to get things done during a difficult time. Did you maintain a positive outlook, or did you struggle with negativity and doubt? How did your mindset impact your actions and decisions, and what strategies can you use to cultivate a more resilient and positive attitude in the face of adversity?

He Will Keep Your Mind

Do not be anxious about anything, but in every situation, by prayer and petition, with thanksgiving, present your requests to God. And the peace of God, which transcends all understanding, will guard your hearts and your minds in Christ Jesus.

— (PHILIPPIANS 4:6-7 NIV)

Losing half your family at any age is not only devastating but also life-changing. The thought of losing a loved one is beyond unfathomable and imaginable. The story of my grandmother losing her family the way she did shocks so many people when they hear of the story. When she would tell the story about how it happened, people looked at her in awe. The look of disbelief at how she was still in her right mind would often draw blank stares and leave people speechless. It had been a story told too often at our home.

The family attended church as a family at 9:00 am until 1:00 pm. After church, they went to the funeral of a family friend's child at 2:00 pm. Once the funeral was over, the family made the usual Sunday afternoon visits in their family station wagon. In the car was my mother and nine of her siblings. The first stop was at my great uncle's house, where my Aunt Velma and Uncle Henry asked to stay over. The second and third stops were at my maternal great-grandmother's and paternal great-grandmother's homes, respectively. It was around 7:00 pm that evening when they arrived home.

Shortly after arriving home, a neighbor visited my grandmother and the newborn baby, Alvin Wayne. It was cold Sunday afternoon, and the house was cold. My Grandfather proceeded to warm the house with the wood stove. As he was getting the fire started, something went terribly wrong. The wood stove caught fire, and the house was in flames. My Grandfather was engulfed in the flames and ran out of the house.

My mother heard the tears and screaming of her younger siblings to help them, but she couldn't get back into the house. She and my uncle Alphonso were at the back of the house near the back door and were able to get out of the house. My mother, age 14, ran after her father, attempting to put the fire out. She was burned on her hands trying to help her father. My uncle Alphonso, age 9, was burned on the side of his face. My Grandfather tried to put himself out of the fire, but it was too late. He had been burned so badly that he had to be hospitalized.

This occurred in 1966. The fire trucks took hours to arrive. By the time they arrived, the two girls, Joann, two years old; Shirley Ann, three years old; Larry, six years old, and three-month-old Alvin Wayne, were pronounced dead on the spot. My Grandfather, 46 years old, died March 8, and my uncle Charles Lewis, 12 years old, died March 7 at UNC Chapel Hill burn center. My mother and uncle were both hospitalized at Cape Fear Valley Hospital, where they remained for weeks for burn treatment and smoke inhalation. My Grandmother was able to escape the fire only because she was standing on the porch saying goodbye to the neighbor who visited the baby.

It would seem that after such a tragic loss, it would give my grandmother no reason to live. She had lost half her family. Her husband, who was the primary breadwinner and confidant to her, was gone. It was enough to make you give up and never have faith again. Yet, she never lost sight of God's grace, mercy, and commitment to her. She was steadfast and immovable in her faith. She lost her home, family, and livelihood, yet she still believed. Her in-laws made all of the funeral arrangements so that she didn't have to. It wasn't that she couldn't; the family thought it might be too much for her to bear and were heartbroken themselves.

Her motto was that she had to keep living. In fact, she told my mother and the other children that she must keep living. Life had to move on. She attributed her mental stamina to God's sovereignty and faithfulness to her. Life has a way of throwing curveballs at you when you least expect it. One moment, everything seems to be going according to plan, and the next, you're caught in a storm you never saw coming. In any situation, your mind must be steadfast and immovable on God's sovereignty and provision.

Grandma Vernesta's Words of Wisdom on being anxious:
"There is no need to be anxious when you
have Jesus in your heart. Our burden is heavy
and his is light. Turn it over to God."

Reflect on Your Journey Trusting God to Keep You Calm:

✐ Reflect on recent situations or thoughts that have triggered anxiety for you. Describe these triggers in detail and explore why they have such an impact on your emotions. Consider strategies you can use to address or mitigate these triggers in the future.

✐ Write about a moment today when you were fully present and at peace. What were you doing, and how did it feel to be completely absorbed in the present moment? Discuss ways you can incorporate more mindfulness practices into your daily routine to reduce anxiety.

✐ Identify a recurring negative thought or belief that contributes to your anxiety. Write about alternative, more balanced perspectives on this thought. How can reframing your thinking help you feel more at ease and less anxious?

✐ Reflect on how you typically respond to yourself when feeling anxious. Are you self-critical or compassionate? Write a letter to yourself from a place of kindness and understanding, offering reassurance and support during times of anxiety.

✐ Develop a personalized relaxation plan that includes activities or strategies you find calming and soothing. Describe each activity in detail and how incorporating them into your routine can help you manage and alleviate anxiety.

CHAPTER 14

Choose Your Words Wisely

*Those who guard their mouths and their
tongues keep themselves from calamity.*

– (PROVERBS 21:23 NIV)

My Grandmother's sister passed away, and the planning of her home-going services presented several challenges. As the eldest sibling, my grandmother took on the responsibility with unwavering resolve. She called her siblings and dictated what needed to happen. Her leadership was decisive and carried out with great care, reflecting her deep sense of duty as the oldest sibling. It wasn't until after her death that I learned about the pivotal role she played during that difficult time. She was a woman of great discretion, choosing not to share what didn't need to be shared. It was simply her way.

My Grandmother's approach to life was always marked by humility and wisdom. She consistently reminded us not to boast about new possessions or accomplishments. Her words were clear: "Don't act like you've never had anything." This was not just advice about humility; it was a way of living that emphasized grace and respect. She ensured that her sister's life was honored in a manner that respectfully represented the life she lived.

Her actions were a powerful reminder of the biblical wisdom found in James, "Everyone should be quick to listen, slow to speak and slow to become angry." (James 1:19 NIV) Even when tempted to react hastily, I pause to reflect on her words and actions. Her life was a testament to the importance of listening more than speaking, acting with integrity, and treating others with the utmost respect.

During the planning of her sister's funeral, my grandmother exhibited incredible strength and composure. Despite the emotional turmoil, she managed to coordinate the details with precision and care. She communicated with each sibling, ensuring that everyone was informed and involved, but she also made it clear what needed to be done. Her ability to take charge in a calm and collected manner was a reflection of her character. She didn't seek recognition for her efforts; she simply did what needed to be done out of love and respect for her sister.

After her death, as we reminisced about her life, I learned more about the quiet strength and discretion she embodied. She never spoke about her own hardships or the challenges she faced. Instead, she focused on helping others and maintaining the dignity of her family. Her discretion wasn't about keeping secrets; it was about respecting the privacy and dignity of others. She understood that some things are best kept within the heart, not out of secrecy but out of respect.

This principle of discretion extended to how she handled the accomplishments and possessions in our family. She taught us to be grateful for what we had without flaunting it. "Don't act like you've never had anything," she would say. This was a lesson in humility, reminding us to appreciate our blessings quietly and without arrogance. Her wisdom in this regard was profound. She knew that true contentment and respect didn't come from showing off what we had but from understanding its value and being grateful.

My Grandmother's philosophy also emphasized the importance of honoring others in a way that reflected their true selves. When planning her sister's funeral, she ensured that every detail was thoughtfully considered. The service was a beautiful tribute that honored her sister's life, values, and the love she shared with her family. It was a testament to my grandmother's understanding of what it means to truly respect and honor someone.

This respect extended beyond just funeral arrangements. It was woven into the fabric of her everyday interactions. She treated everyone with kindness and respect, regardless of their background or circumstances. She believed in the inherent worth of every person and acted accordingly. Her actions taught me the value of treating others with dignity and compassion, a lesson that has stayed with me throughout my life.

Her teachings have guided me in my own life, especially when faced with situations that test my patience and understanding. I remember her words and actions whenever I am tempted to react impulsively. I think about the wisdom in being "quick to hear, slow to speak, slow to anger." This biblical advice, combined with her example, has helped me navigate many difficult situations with grace and composure.

Reflecting on her life and the impact she had on me, I am reminded of the profound wisdom in her seemingly simple advice. Her insistence on humility, respect, and discretion was not just about maintaining appearances; they were about cultivating a deeper understanding of what it means to live a meaningful and honorable life. She understood that our actions and words have a lasting impact, and she lived her life in a way that reflected this understanding.

Her legacy continues to influence me in ways I never fully appreciated until after her passing. I hope to pass on the values she taught me to future generations. Her wisdom and strength have become a guiding light in my life, helping me navigate challenges with grace and purpose. Whenever I am faced with a difficult decision or a moment of doubt, I think of her and the lessons she taught me.

**Grandma Vernesta's Words of
Wisdom on Talking Too Much:**

*"Keep your mouth closed. Sometimes, silence is the best
answer. It's not good to run your mouth all the time."*

Reflect on Your Journey on Discretion:

- Reflect on a recent conversation where you felt you talked more than necessary. What were the circumstances that led to this? How did you feel during and after the conversation? Consider what you could have done differently to balance the conversation more effectively.

- Choose a conversation or interaction you have planned for today. Before the conversation begins, set an intention to actively listen more and speak less. Journal about your experience afterward. How did the conversation flow differently when you focused on listening? What insights did you gain by allowing the other person more space to speak?

- Spend 10-15 minutes observing a group conversation without actively participating. Write about what you noticed during this time. How did the dynamics of the conversation change when you were less involved? What did you learn about the flow of conversation and the contributions of different participants?

- Reflect on a time when you practiced mindful communication—speaking intentionally and purposefully. Describe the impact this had on the quality of your interactions. How can you incorporate more mindful communication techniques into your daily conversations to ensure you speak only when necessary?

- Before entering a social or professional setting, set an intention to speak less and listen more. Journal about how you maintained this intention throughout the interaction. What strategies did you use to resist the urge to speak unnecessarily? Reflect on the outcomes of this intentional speaking approach.

CHAPTER 15

Everyone In Church Ain't Saved

Not everyone who says to me, 'Lord, Lord,' will enter the kingdom of heaven, but only the one who does the will of my Father who is in heaven.

— (MATTHEW 7:21 NIV)

Growing up in the Bible Belt, attending church was a lifestyle. There seemed to be a church on every corner. Our family friends were members of the current church or previous churches that we had been a member of in the past. They became family. In my young mind, I thought individuals who went to church and shouted "Praise the Lord" were free from sin, wrongdoings, or mistakes. In my mind, I put them on a pedestal. I thought that your church attendance meant perfection. It would be hard for me to believe that if you attended church, you would be mean, lie, or even steal from anyone. This was engrained in my brain.

The notion that the extent of kindness or moral behavior directly correlates with one's level of church attendance was completely false. I learned that people's behavior is influenced by some factors, including personal values, upbringing, and individual choices rather than their religious participation. While many individuals attending church embody kindness and compassion, no community is immune to encountering individuals who may display unkind or mean behavior.

Like any other social group, church communities consist of diverse individuals with varying personalities, perspectives, and life experiences. There will be instances of unkindness that can stem from personal struggles, misunderstandings, or conflicts. She would often say that it doesn't matter how often someone attends church or says Lord, Lord, it doesn't mean that they are living their life as God intends them to live it. The takeaway from this parable was that no one belonged on a pedestal or was free from hurting other people.

My Grandmother was extremely careful about putting churchgoers on pedestals. She would often gather us around and, in her gentle yet firm voice, remind us of an essential truth: "We are all human and fall short of the glory of God." Her wisdom stemmed from years of observing the world around her, and she understood the dangers of idealizing those who appeared devout. She emphasized that while respect for everyone was paramount, we must also acknowledge that people make mistakes, and it did no good to think of churchgoers as higher than ourselves.

Grandmother's perspective was rooted in a deep and abiding faith. She believed that true spirituality was not about public displays of piety but the sincerity of one's heart and actions. "Everyone that reads the Bible isn't going to go to Heaven," she would say, her eyes reflecting both conviction and compassion. This statement often surprised those who heard it, as it challenged the notion that religious rituals and church attendance were enough to secure one's place in the afterlife.

For her, the essence of faith lay in the teachings of Jesus Christ and living one's life according to His will. "You must have Jesus deep in your heart," she would tell us, "And live your life according to His will to truly have salvation." This meant that our actions, decisions, and the way we treated others were far more significant than merely attending church services or reciting scriptures.

Grandmother's teachings instilled in us a profound sense of humility. She made us understand that no one was infallible, and even those who seemed devout could falter. This view was particularly enlightening because it encouraged us to focus on our own spiritual growth rather than judging or comparing ourselves to others. It also taught us to be forgiving and understanding, recognizing that everyone has their own struggles and shortcomings.

Her message was one of inclusivity and compassion. She highlighted our shared humanity by asserting that everyone falls short of God's glory. This understanding fostered a sense of community and empathy, reminding us that we are all on a spiritual journey together. It also underscored the importance of supporting one another rather than competing or seeking to outshine others in our faith.

Grandmother's caution against idolizing churchgoers was also a call for authenticity. She valued genuine faith and integrity over outward appearances. In her eyes, a humble heart that sought to follow Jesus's teachings was far more valuable than any public display of religiosity. This perspective encouraged us to cultivate a personal and sincere relationship with God rather than focusing on how others perceived our faith.

Moreover, her emphasis on living according to Jesus's will provides a clear and actionable guide for our lives. It was not enough to profess faith; we had to live it out in our daily actions. This included acts of kindness, forgiveness, and love—values that Jesus exemplified. By following His example, we could strive to embody the true essence of Christianity.

Grandmother's wisdom also served as a reminder of the pitfalls of hypocrisy. She had seen how easy it was for people to hide behind a façade of piety while neglecting the core tenets of their faith. Her teachings urged us to be wary of such behavior and strive for congruence between our beliefs and actions. This meant being honest with ourselves about our flaws and working continuously to align our lives with Jesus's teachings.

Her perspective on salvation was both sobering and inspiring. It reminded us that spiritual growth was an ongoing process and that we could always strive to deepen our faith and improve our actions. Her belief that having Jesus deep in our hearts was crucial for salvation emphasized the importance of an internal transformation—a change that went beyond external rituals and was reflected in our daily lives.

In essence, Grandmother's teachings were a profound guide for living a meaningful and spiritually fulfilling life. She taught us to respect and love others, to be humble and authentic, and to seek a deep and sincere relationship with God. Her wisdom continues to resonate, reminding us that true faith is not about perfection or outward appearances but about the sincerity of our hearts and the alignment of our lives with the teachings of Jesus. Through her guidance, we learned that living according to God's will and having Jesus deeply embedded in our hearts are the true paths to salvation.

Grandma Vernesta's Words of Wisdom about Church folk:

"Everyone in Church Ain't Saved."

Reflect on Your Journey:

- Reflect on what it means to have true faith and a genuine relationship with God. How do you distinguish between outward religious practices and inward spiritual transformation? Write about your own experiences and observations in your faith community.

- Consider your own spiritual journey and relationship with God. How do you ensure that your faith is genuine and not just a series of rituals or routines? Reflect on ways to deepen your connection with God beyond attending church services.

- Think about the difference between authentic worship and going through the motions. How can you cultivate a more sincere and heartfelt worship experience for yourself? Write about the steps you can take to ensure your worship is genuine and not just a habitual practice.

- Reflect on the idea of judging others' faith and spiritual journeys. How can you foster a more compassionate and understanding attitude toward others in your faith community?

- Write about the signs of genuine spiritual transformation you have observed in yourself or others. How do these signs differ from merely attending church services? Reflect on how you can encourage and support authentic spiritual growth within your church community.

CHAPTER 16

Anything Is Possible with God

*I can do all this through him
who gives me strength.*

— (PHILIPPIANS 4:13 NIV)

I was riding with my mother in the car some time ago, and we discussed my childhood. She, my daughter, and I were together, and my daughter asked her what it was like raising me as a child. My mother chuckled and replied, "She was a lot like you, actually. I never had to spank her; she always listened and was never afraid of anything." She proceeded to share this story about how I learned how to swim.

Before telling the story, she asked me how I learned how to swim because I did not take lessons, and she was nowhere around when I learned how to swim. Interestingly, my mother was fearful of the water and attempted to raise my siblings and me the same way. While we frequented the beaches and lakes in the south, she would always be extremely cautious about the water. Often screaming and yelling out not to go so far out. I don't think she ever felt settled with us being in the water. She told my daughter, "Your mother was always brave, and she learned how to do things without me." At that moment, I don't think I had ever heard my mother articulate how I operated as a child.

I began to share with them how I learned how to swim. I was eight years old at a friend's house, and they had a pool. The visit was planned, and I knew we would go swimming when I visited. However, I had not been to the pool without my parents. My friend's house was within walking distance and in the same neighborhood as ours. I could've walked, but my mother decided to drive me. She wanted to make sure I understood the pool rules, such as don't jump in, don't go underwater, stay on the side, make sure there is an adult outside with you, and so on and so forth. I yes ma'amed her the whole ride there. We arrived, and my mother said, "Don't forget what I told you."

My friend and I went out to the pool, and I was sheepishly holding on to the side. I was kicking the water as if I knew what to do. I leaned my head back into the water as I watched her jump in and out of the pool, splashing and enjoying the pool time. A few minutes later, she said, "You don't know how to swim". I said, "Yes, I do."

I began to tell her how fearful my mother was of the water, and because she wasn't there, she wanted me to be extremely careful. I figured that would be enough to stop her from asking me if I could swim or not. It didn't stop her from asking. Her next question to me was to show me. I dare you to jump in the deep end. I did not hesitate to get out of the water to show her.

I don't recall if that was my opportunity to jump in the water as my mother had asked me not to or if I was too prideful to tell her I really couldn't swim. No matter what it was, I wasn't afraid. I figured I could do the same since I had watched her jump in and out of the water and she was still alive. I didn't worry about my hair or if I would even drown. I released all inhibitions. I knew I could do it, so I bravely replied, yes, I can, held my breath, and jumped in.

When I emerged from underwater, she said, "Wow, I hadn't ever jumped in the deep in before." As I reflected on this, the nostalgic corridors of memory of my childhood fearlessness emerged as a part of who I was and who I am today.

Teaching myself how to swim and conquer a fear that was not my own, was not my only experience of being a daredevil. I often jumped off rooftops with my brother and male cousins and rode bikes down a steep hill with no hands and not peddling. The threads of audacity, boundless curiosity, and an irrepressible sense of adventure were present in me. Those carefree days were marked by a willingness to plunge into the unknown, fueled by an insatiable desire to explore, learn, and conquer.

As the years unfolded, that fearless essence didn't dissipate; instead, it evolved. The daring leaps from playground structures became metaphorical jumps into the realms of adulthood—bold decisions, career pursuits, and personal challenges. The same courage that prompted me to climb trees and cross imaginary boundaries now propels me to scale the peaks of my ambitions and confront the complexities of grown-up responsibilities.

My childhood fearlessness, once manifested in scraped knees and giggles, has matured into a formidable force. I learned from these experiences that fearlessness is the driving energy behind my resilience, enabling me to face adversities with a determined gaze and transform setbacks into lessons. Like a compass, fearlessness directs you through the uncharted territories of adulthood, turning uncertainties into opportunities and shaping your narrative with an unwavering spirit.

In a world that often demands caution, your fearlessness is a reminder that embracing challenges with an open heart can lead to extraordinary growth. As you navigate the intricate dance of life, your inner child's fearless spirit continues to be a source of inspiration, guiding you toward a future where each step is taken with the same daring enthusiasm that marked your earliest adventures.

**Grandma Vernesta's Words of
Wisdom on people doubting you:**

*"Sometimes you have to encourage yourself. Don't
worry about what other people say; as long as
you have Jesus, everything will be alright."*

Reflect on Your Journey:

- Recall a specific instance when someone doubted your abilities or decisions. How did their doubt make you feel, and what motivated you to keep believing in yourself despite their skepticism? Write about the steps you took to overcome their doubt and prove them wrong.

- Reflect on where your inner strength and self-belief come from. How have these qualities helped you in situations where others doubted you? Describe a time when your self-confidence made a significant difference in achieving your goals.

- Think about the people who have supported and believed in you when others did not. How did their support influence your ability to persevere? Write about the impact these supportive individuals have had on your journey and how you can cultivate a positive support system in the future.

- List some of your proudest achievements that you accomplished despite others' doubts. How did believing in yourself contribute to these successes? Reflect on how these experiences have shaped your resilience and self-assurance.

- Consider the lessons you have learned from situations where people doubted you. How have these experiences helped you grow personally and professionally? Write about how you can apply these lessons to future challenges and continue to trust in your own capabilities.

CHAPTER

17

Everyone Can't Go

*One who has unreliable friends soon
comes to ruin, but there is a friend
who sticks closer than a brother.*

— (PROVERBS 18:24 NIV)

God removes people from your life because He heard conversations that you didn't hear. This truth has become increasingly evident to me over the years, particularly through experiences where I realized that not everyone in my corner was genuinely supportive. Often, these individuals would smile and cheer me on, but their hearts were not aligned with their outward expressions. Eventually, these people seemed to move further and further away. The phone calls stopped, the invitations ceased, and social media told the story of their lives continuing without me. It was a painful realization that the people I thought I knew had become strangers.

The late great Dr. Maya Angelou said, "When people show you who they are the first time, believe them." Early on, I couldn't fathom the truth of this statement, but over time, I have become wiser and more accepting of it. It's not always about what I've done; sometimes, it's just about who people are. God knew it was time for those relationships to end, as their reason or season in my life had come to a close.

Reflecting on these experiences, I can now see the wisdom in God's timing and His way of orchestrating events in our lives. There were moments when I felt deeply hurt and confused by the sudden distance of friends or acquaintances. It felt like a betrayal, especially when I had done nothing to warrant their withdrawal. But with time and perspective, I began to understand that God was protecting me from unseen harm. He had heard conversations and witnessed actions that I was unaware of, and in His infinite wisdom, He removed those individuals from my life for my own good.

One particular instance stands out vividly in my memory. I had a close friend who I believed was supportive and genuinely happy about my successes. We would share our dreams and encourage each other. However, as I began to achieve some of my goals, I noticed a subtle shift in our relationship. She became distant, and our conversations grew strained. Eventually, the calls and invitations stopped altogether. I found out through social media that she was hosting events and gatherings without me. It was a painful revelation that someone I considered a friend was no longer interested in being a part of my life.

At first, I was devastated. I questioned myself and replayed our interactions, trying to pinpoint what I might have done wrong. However, as I reflected on Dr. Maya Angelou's wisdom, I realized that this person had shown me who she was long before the final break. I had brushed off moments of jealousy and competitiveness, thinking they were minor issues. But those moments were glimpses into her true feelings, and I had ignored them. When she finally distanced herself, it was God's way of removing her from my life because He knew what I couldn't see.

This experience taught me a valuable lesson about trust and discernment. It's crucial to pay attention to the subtle signs that people give us about their true intentions. We often want to see the best in those around us, but sometimes, we must accept that not everyone is meant to stay in our lives forever. People come into our lives for reasons and seasons, and when their purpose is fulfilled, it's okay to let them go. Holding on to relationships that God is trying to end can hinder our growth and keep us from the blessings He has in store for us.

People change over time. They grow, evolve, and sometimes, they grow apart. It's a natural part of life's journey. Just as trees in the fall shed their leaves to prepare for new growth, we too, must sometimes shed relationships that no longer serve us or align with our paths. The good news is that God knows this long before we do. He understands the ebb and flow of relationships and guides us through the seasons of our lives, even when we can't see the full picture ourselves.

Reflecting on my own life, I've experienced the pain and confusion of relationships changing and people drifting away. Friends who once felt like family have become distant, and connections that seemed unbreakable have dissolved. At first, it was difficult to accept. I wondered what went wrong and questioned if I had done something to cause the separation. But with time, I began to understand that this process of shedding relationships is necessary for personal growth and spiritual alignment.

I wanted to believe the best in everyone and thought that time and effort could mend any relationship. But as I grew wiser, I began to embrace this truth. It wasn't about what I had done but about who these people were and the role they were meant to play in my life. God knew it was time for these relationships to end, and I had to trust His judgment.

Each step along this journey was a testament to God's plan for my life. The people who left, the opportunities that fell through, and the new paths that opened were all part of His design. I learned to trust that when relationships end, it's often because they've served their purpose in our lives. Just like trees shedding leaves in the fall, we must let go to make room for new growth.

Through these experiences, I've learned that it's okay to let people go. Relationships that once felt essential may no longer fit as we grow and change. It's not a failure or a reflection of inadequacy. Instead, it's a natural part of life's progression. By holding on to relationships that God is trying to end, we can hinder our own growth and miss out on the new blessings He has in store for us.

Accepting this truth has brought a sense of peace and clarity to my life. I now view the end of relationships not as losses but as opportunities for new beginnings. When people show who they truly are, I believe them and adjust my expectations accordingly. This approach has allowed me to cultivate more authentic and supportive connections.

God's timing is perfect, even when it doesn't align with our own plans. He knows the conversations and intentions we are unaware of, and He protects us, even if it means removing people from our lives. When I reflect on the friends who have drifted away, I realize that their departure made space for new, more meaningful relationships.

People change over time. They grow and sometimes grow apart, and that's okay. Life does that, and just like trees in the fall shedding leaves, we have to shed some relationships. The good news is that God knows this before we do. By trusting in His plan and embracing the changes that come our way, we can navigate life's transitions with grace and confidence. God removes people from our lives because He hears conversations we do not. He sees the bigger picture and knows what is best for us. As we trust in His guidance and let go of what no longer serves us, we make room for new growth and blessings.

Life is a series of seasons, each with its own purpose and beauty. By accepting the natural ebb and flow of relationships, we can move forward with a sense of peace and purpose. God's plan is always for our highest good, and when we trust in Him, we find that every change, every goodbye, and every new beginning is a step toward becoming the people we are meant to be.

To Everything There Is a Season

(Ecclesiastes 3:1-8 NIV)

To everything there is a season,
And a time for every purpose under heaven:
A time to be born and a time to die,
A time to plant and a time to uproot,
A time to kill and a time to heal,
A time to break down and a time to build,
A time to weep and a time to laugh,
A time to mourn and a time to dance,
A time to cast away stones and a time
to gather stones together,
A time to embrace and a time to refrain from embracing,
A time to search and a time to count as lost,
A time to keep and a time to discard,
A time to tear and a time to mend,
A time to be silent and a time to speak,
a time to love and a time to hate,
A time for war and a time for peace.

Grandma Vernesta's Words of Wisdom in choosing friends:
*"Not everyone who says they are your friend is your friend.
You have to move on and leave people where they are."*

Reflect on Your Journey:

- Reflect on the qualities that make someone a true friend. Write about a time when you realized that not everyone in your circle had your best interests at heart. How did you distinguish between true friends and those who were not? What qualities do you value most in a friendship?

- Think about a situation where you felt betrayed by someone you considered a friend. How did this experience impact your view on friendship? What lessons did you learn from this experience about trust and loyalty? How has it influenced the way you choose your friends now?

- Consider the importance of setting boundaries in relationships. Write about a time when setting boundaries helped you protect your emotional well-being. How do you ensure that the people you allow into your inner circle respect these boundaries?

- Reflect on the idea that not everyone can go with you on your journey. Write about a specific instance where you had to distance yourself from someone to achieve your goals or maintain your peace. How did making this choice benefit your personal growth and well-being?

- Take a moment to evaluate your current relationships. Are there people in your life who may not have your best interests at heart? Write about how you can gently distance yourself from negative influences and focus on nurturing relationships that support and uplift you.

Swing For the Fences

Whatever you do, work at it with all your heart,
as working for the Lord, not for human masters.

– (COLOSSIANS 3:23 NIV)

I always believed in myself. There was something inside of me that told me I could do anything, no matter what it was. Whether it was sports or climbing trees, I always thought I could do it just as well as, or even better than, the boys. I recall once someone telling me that I was the kind of person who thought I could do anything but that I didn't do anything right, and everything I had done had failed.

My first thought was that it's best not to respond. My second thought was that the God I serve would give me my heart's desires, and it would be by His strength and might, not mine. The scripture that came to mind was Philippians: "I can do all this through Him who gives me strength." (Philippians 4:13 NIV) Lastly, I chuckled on the inside because they didn't realize the strength that I had built was not of my own.

Reflecting on those words, I understood that their assessment of my failures was superficial, missing the depth of my journey and the source of my perseverance. My faith was my anchor, the silent force that propelled me forward even in the face of adversity. I realized that the successes I sought weren't always visible to others; they were milestones of personal growth, resilience, and unwavering faith. Each challenge was a steppingstone, and every failure was a lesson that brought me closer to realizing my true potential.

This strength, born from a place of deep belief and spiritual fortitude, allowed me to transcend the limitations imposed by others. I was not merely striving to prove my worth but to fulfill a purpose that was greater than myself. This inner conviction, bolstered by my faith, made me unstoppable.

In moments of doubt or criticism, I turned inward, drawing on the wellspring of courage and determination that my faith provided. It wasn't about the external validation or the immediate successes; it was about the journey

Funeral Home photo of the five children and husband

and the unwavering belief that I could do all things through Christ who strengthened me. And so, with each step, I moved forward, not deterred by the naysayers but motivated by a higher calling and the inner voice that reminded me of the limitless possibilities that lay ahead.

Being told that I would not likely measure up fueled my confidence. I had to see myself within and feel the accomplishment. I didn't grow up with a silver spoon and had to work hard to get to where I am today. It was the good old-fashioned hard work—no handouts, but tangible hard work that forced me to learn and grow. I never wanted to settle, and I never wanted the people around me to settle. I was also fearless. I felt the butterflies, but I jumped in headfirst time and time again. I didn't care about the thoughts of others; what mattered was that I gave it my all and that I tried. Each challenge was a testament to my resilience, a proving ground where I could test my limits and push beyond them.

The journey wasn't easy. There were countless obstacles, moments of doubt, and setbacks that could have easily derailed my progress. But instead of succumbing to these challenges, I used them to fuel my determination. The more people doubted me, the more determined I became to prove them wrong. Their skepticism became the catalyst for my perseverance.

I understood early on that success wasn't just about talent or opportunity; it was about the relentless pursuit of my goals, no matter how insurmountable they seemed. Hard work became my mantra, and with every effort, I built a foundation of experience and wisdom that no one could take away from me. This foundation was not just built on achievements but on the lessons learned from every failure and setback.

Fearlessness was my ally. I embraced every opportunity with open arms, ready to face whatever came my way. The butterflies in my stomach were not signs of fear but indicators of my courage. They reminded me that I was alive, striving, and pushing the boundaries of my comfort zone. Each leap of faith was a testament to my belief in myself and my capabilities.

I was never content with mediocrity, and I encouraged those around me to adopt the same mindset. Settling was never an option; there was always another goal to achieve, another milestone to reach. My journey was as much about inspiring others as it was about achieving personal success. I wanted to show that anything was possible with hard work, determination, and a fearless attitude.

In the end, it wasn't just about proving others wrong; it was about proving to myself that I could rise above any challenge. It was about the satisfaction of knowing that I had given my all, faced my fears head-on, and never settled for less than my best. This relentless drive, this refusal to settle, is what propelled me forward and continues to fuel my journey today.

Strive for excellence in everything that you do. Even if it means staying up a little longer or adding a few extra hours to your efforts, give it your all. I wanted to hit a home run every day. I believe people deserve your best, and you should always be your best. Your efforts determine your outcomes.

Excellence isn't about perfection but a commitment to giving your utmost in every endeavor. This mindset transforms ordinary tasks into opportunities for growth and success. Each moment becomes a chance to push your limits, to learn, and to excel. Whether you're working on a project, nurturing relationships, or pursuing personal goals, striving for excellence ensures that you are always moving forward and always improving.

When you dedicate yourself to excellence, you develop a work ethic that sets you apart. It's easy to settle for mediocrity, to do just enough to get by. But true fulfillment comes from knowing that you've given your best, regardless of the result. This dedication is evident in the quality of your work, how you approach challenges, and the respect you earn from others.

There will be times when striving for excellence requires sacrifices. Late nights, early mornings, and extra hours of effort are often necessary. These sacrifices are not in vain; they are investments in your future. Each extra hour, each additional effort, is a step closer to achieving your goals. It's during these moments of dedication that you build resilience and character, qualities that will serve you well in all aspects of life.

I wanted to hit a home run every day, not just for personal satisfaction but because I believe people deserve your best. When you give your all, you inspire those around you. Your dedication sets a standard, creating a culture of excellence that motivates others to also give their best. This ripple effect can transform teams, organizations, and communities, driving everyone toward greater success.

Your efforts determine your outcomes. While external factors can influence results, the level of effort you put in is something you can control. You increase the likelihood of achieving your desired outcomes by consistently striving for excellence. Success often results from hard work, persistence, and a relentless pursuit of high standards.

It's important to remember that striving for excellence is a journey, not a destination. There will be setbacks and failures along the way, but these are merely opportunities to learn and grow. Each challenge you face is a test of your commitment to excellence. How you respond to these challenges defines your character and determines your path forward.

In striving for excellence, you also cultivate a sense of pride and self-respect. Knowing that you've given your best effort boosts your confidence and self-esteem. It reinforces the belief that you are capable of achieving great things. This positive mindset is crucial for overcoming obstacles and reaching new heights.

Moreover, excellence is about more than just achieving goals; it's about the process. It's about taking pride in your work, finding joy in the journey, and appreciating the progress you make along the way. When you focus on the process, you become more resilient and adaptable, better equipped to handle the inevitable ups and downs of life.

So, strive for excellence in everything that you do. Commit to giving your best effort, no matter the task. Stay up a little longer, add those extra hours, and push yourself beyond your comfort zone. Aim to hit a home run every day. Remember that people deserve your best, and you deserve to be your best. Your efforts will determine your outcomes, and through a steadfast commitment to excellence, you will achieve the success you seek.

Determination at a Track meet while at NC A&T State University

**Grandma Vernesta's Words of Wisdom
on Setting Your Sights High:**
*"Do things in excellence and to the absolute best of your
abilities. Don't take any shortcuts."*

Reflect on Your Journey of Reaching Your Goals:

- Reflect on what "excellence" means to you in various aspects of your life, work, personal goals, relationships, etc. Write about specific actions or habits that you believe exemplify doing things to the best of your abilities. How do you maintain high standards in your daily tasks?

- Think about when you were tempted to take a shortcut in a project or task. What were the circumstances, and what decision did you ultimately make? Reflect on the outcome and how taking the high road impacted the quality of your work and your personal integrity.

- Identify a person or several people you believe embody the principle of doing things excellently. What qualities do they possess, and how do they inspire you? Write about specific instances where their actions have motivated you to avoid shortcuts and strive for excellence in your own life.

- Set specific goals for yourself that involve achieving excellence in your current projects or endeavors. Write about the steps you plan to take to meet these goals without compromising on quality or integrity. How will you measure your success and stay motivated to maintain high standards?

- Think back to a project or task where you put in your absolute best effort and avoided any shortcuts. Describe the process and the final outcome. How did it feel to see the results of your hard work and dedication? Reflect on how this experience reinforces the value of consistently striving for excellence in all you do.

chapter 19

Trust in God for Your Mate

Take delight in the LORD, and he will
give you the desires of your heart.

– (PSALMS 37:4 NIV)

Finding love in the most unusual ways seems to be a pattern of mine. I used to pray that God would send someone who could live a life that would bring me closer to Him. In time, I met the most amazing man who met me right where I needed to be. I wanted a Southern man who worked hard, had great values, and would love my children. God gave me more than that. The protector, provider, and friend I longed for seemed to be waiting for me at the right place and at the right time.

My goal was to slowly walk this relationship, but we soon became inseparable. I was not expecting or looking for any type of relationship and had intended to take time for myself. Yet, I accepted God's timing and not my own for this. The circumstances were different because I now had two children to consider, and I was very protective of who and what I exposed them to.

Chivalry was not dead. He opened every door, pulled out chairs, and drove on long road trips. The level of respect he showed for me was absolutely incredible and refreshing. Most importantly, he loved God. He was confident in my positions and allowed me to shine. He was well accomplished and didn't hesitate to champion me.

Reflecting on our journey, I see how every prayer and every hope I had was answered in ways I couldn't have imagined. This relationship wasn't just about finding love; it was about finding a partner who aligned with my deepest values and aspirations. He brought out the best in me, supported me unconditionally, and became an integral part of me and my children's lives.

Navigating this new chapter, I appreciated how effortlessly he integrated into our family. He treated my children with the same love and care he showed me, strengthening our bond. His presence brought a sense of security and stability that I had longed for. Every act of kindness and respect he displayed reinforced my belief that true, godly love still existed.

We shared a mutual respect for each other's independence and strengths. He encouraged my ambitions and celebrated my successes, never feeling threatened by them. Instead, he stood beside me as my biggest supporter, always ready to uplift and inspire. His confidence in my abilities and his unwavering faith in our relationship created a solid foundation for us to build upon.

This relationship taught me the beauty of trusting in God's timing. The love we found was not forced or rushed; it was a divine alignment of our paths. We grew together, learned from each other, and built a partnership grounded in faith and mutual respect. This journey taught me that when we let go of our own timelines and expectations and trust in God's plan, we often find blessings far greater than we ever imagined.

Allow yourself to love again. Release any strongholds that could be preventing you from loving yourself and anyone else who is so deserving. Someone needs you, and you need you. Don't allow the bitterness to seep into the fabric of who you are. If it feels like it is, force yourself to release it. There is so much to be found in the release. God is love, and love heals and gives us a window into peace and hope.

In life, we often build walls around our hearts to protect ourselves from pain. These walls, however, can become prisons that keep us from experiencing the profound joy and fulfillment that love brings. It's easy to hold on to past hurts and disappointments, letting them shape our outlook and actions. But to truly live, we must let go of these strongholds.

Releasing the grip of bitterness and resentment is not a sign of weakness; it's a testament to your strength and resilience. It takes courage to confront the things that have hurt you and to make a conscious decision to let them go. Doing so opens space for new possibilities and allows love to flow freely into your life.

Self-love is the cornerstone of this transformation. When you learn to love yourself, you set the standard for how others should treat you. You recognize your worth and refuse to settle for anything less than you deserve. This self-love radiates outward, attracting people who appreciate and value you for who you are.

Remember, someone out there needs you just as much as you need yourself. Your unique qualities, kindness, and strength are all needed in this world. When you embrace love, you become a beacon of hope and inspiration for others. Your willingness to love again can spark a chain reaction, encouraging those around you to do the same.

If you ever feel bitterness starting to weave into your being, take proactive steps to release it. Engage in activities that bring you joy and peace. Surround yourself with positive influences. Reflect on the blessings in your life and the lessons learned from past experiences. Each step you take towards releasing negativity brings you closer to a life filled with love and happiness.

God is love, and through Him, we find the strength to heal and move forward. Love is a divine gift that offers us a glimpse of serenity and hope. It reminds us that we are never alone, we are cherished, and there is always a brighter tomorrow.

In allowing yourself to love again, you embrace the fullness of life. You become open to the beauty and wonder that love brings. You give yourself permission to experience joy and to share it with others. Love has the power to heal wounds, bridge gaps, and create bonds that withstand the test of time. So, take that leap of faith. Trust in the process of healing and growth. Allow love to permeate every aspect of your being, knowing that it is through love that we find true peace and fulfillment. Release any strongholds, embrace the possibilities, and let love guide you to a brighter, more hopeful future.

Grandma Vernesta's Words of Wisdom on Finding Love:
*"God will bring you your mate. It is important
to be equally yoked. Don't rush because you
might end up with the wrong person."*

Reflect on Your Love Journey:

- ✐ What core values and priorities are most important to you in a relationship? How do these align with what you seek in a partner?

- ✐ What qualities or traits are non-negotiable for you in a partner? Why are these aspects critical for a successful relationship?

- ✐ How do you envision effective communication and conflict resolution in a relationship? What strategies do you consider important for maintaining healthy interactions?

- ✐ What shared goals and vision do you hope to have with a partner? How do you see these shared aspirations contributing to a fulfilling partnership?

- ✐ What does emotional support look like for you in a relationship? How can you ensure that you and your partner feel supported and understood?

Sometimes You Have to Encourage Yourself

For the Spirit God gave us does not make us timid, but gives us power, love, and self-discipline.

– (2 TIMOTHY 1:7 NIV)

Reclaim the power within by any means necessary. Fight until you can't fight anymore. Find the center of who you were before losing your way. I had become a wife, mom, and executive in a matter of months. As days went by, I became a distant thought of who I was. I wasn't giving myself any room for error. I stopped doing things that made me happy before the titles. I would look back, and there I stood, like a shell of a person. I had allowed the words of others and the box that I was put in to shape who I was. One day, I woke up, snapped out of the fog, and fought like hell to get back the person, dreams, and toughness that had become an afterthought.

In the whirlwind of becoming a wife, mom, and executive, I lost sight of my true self. Each role demanded so much of me that I barely had time to catch my breath, let alone reflect on who I was or what I wanted. The weight of expectations pressed down on me from every direction. Society had clear ideas about what a wife should be, what a mom should do, and how an executive should act. Caught in the crossfire of these expectations, I found myself conforming to each role, slowly erasing the essence of who I was.

I began my days early, juggling the demands of my household and my career. Mornings were a blur of preparing breakfast, getting the kids ready for school, and rushing to meet work deadlines. By evening, I was exhausted, barely able to keep my eyes open, let alone spend quality time with my family or engage in activities that brought me joy. Weekends were no different, filled with chores, errands, and a never-ending to-do list. Amidst all this, the vibrant, passionate person I once was faded into the background.

It wasn't just the physical exhaustion but the mental and emotional toll that was the hardest to bear. I began to internalize the criticism and unsolicited advice from others. Every comment about my parenting, work, or appearance chipped away at my self-esteem. I became hyper-aware of my perceived shortcomings, constantly striving for unattainable perfection. The pressure to be the perfect wife, the perfect mom, and the perfect executive became overwhelming.

I stopped giving myself room for error. There was no space for mistakes or failures in my tightly controlled life. Any deviation from the plan felt like a personal failure. This relentless pursuit of perfection was exhausting and unsustainable. It left no room for spontaneity, creativity, or joy. The hobbies and interests that once brought me happiness were pushed aside and sacrificed on the altar of my new responsibilities.

I would look in the mirror and see a stranger staring back at me. The person I had become was far from the passionate, driven individual I once was. I missed the days when I could lose myself in a good book, paint for hours, or take long walks without a care in the world. I missed the freedom of being myself, unencumbered by the weight of expectations.

The turning point came one morning when I woke up feeling more exhausted than usual. A wave of realization washed over me as I lay in bed, staring at the ceiling. I had become a shell of a person, going through the motions without truly living.

The spark that once ignited my soul had dimmed, replaced by a monotonous routine. I knew something had to change. I needed to reclaim the power within me to fight for the person I had lost.

Reclaiming that power was not easy. It required confronting the parts of myself that I had ignored or suppressed. It meant facing the fears and insecurities that had kept me trapped in a cycle of self-doubt and perfectionism. I began by setting boundaries and prioritizing self-care. I carved out time for myself, even if it was just a few minutes each day. I rediscovered the activities that brought me joy and made them a non-negotiable part of my routine.

I also had to challenge the negative self-talk that had taken root in my mind. I replaced self-criticism with self-compassion, reminding myself that it was okay to make mistakes and that I was deserving of love and respect, just as I was. I sought support from friends, family, and a therapist, who helped me navigate this journey of self-discovery and healing.

As I fought to reclaim my identity, I noticed a shift in my perspective. I began to see the beauty in imperfection and the strength in vulnerability. I realized that my worth was not defined by my roles or the opinions of others but by the person I was at my core. The process was gradual, but I felt a little more like myself with each step.

I learned to balance my responsibilities without losing sight of who I was. I became more present in my relationships, more engaged in my work, and more connected to my passions. I found joy in the simple things and took pride in my accomplishments, no matter how small. I stopped comparing myself to others and focused on my own journey.

Reclaiming my power also meant redefining success. Instead of striving for an unattainable ideal, I set realistic and meaningful goals. I celebrated progress rather than perfection and embraced the journey rather than just the destination. This shift in mindset allowed me to approach life with a sense of curiosity and openness rather than fear and anxiety.

I also learned to say no. Saying no to things that drained my energy or didn't align with my values was liberating. It created space for the things that truly mattered to me and allowed me to invest my time and energy in ways that were fulfilling. I stopped trying to please everyone and focused on what was best for me and my family.

The journey to reclaim my power was not linear. There were setbacks and moments of doubt, but each challenge strengthened my resolve. I learned to trust myself and my instincts and to listen to my inner voice rather than the noise of external expectations. Before losing my way, I found the center of who I was and embraced that person with all my flaws and strengths.

Through this process, I discovered a newfound sense of resilience and confidence. I became more assertive, standing up for myself and my needs. I realized that reclaiming my power was not about being perfect or having it all together but about being authentic and true to myself. It was about embracing my journey, with all its highs and lows, and finding strength in my vulnerability.

Reclaiming my power also meant reconnecting with my dreams. I revisited the aspirations and passions that had been sidelined and made a conscious effort to pursue them. I set new goals and worked towards them with determination and enthusiasm. This renewed focus on my dreams brought a sense of purpose and fulfillment that had been missing for so long.

As I reclaimed my power, I noticed a positive impact on my relationships. I became more present and engaged with my family, nurturing our connections with love and intention. I approached my role as an executive with a fresh perspective, leading with empathy and authenticity. The balance I found within myself translated into a more balanced and harmonious life overall.

Reclaiming my power within was an act of self-love and self-respect. It was a declaration that I was worthy of happiness, fulfillment, and success on my own terms. It reminded me that I had the strength and resilience to overcome any obstacle and that my worth was not defined by external validation but by my own belief in myself.

As I continue this journey, I am committed to nurturing my power and staying true to myself. I am determined to live a life that is aligned with my values, passions, and dreams. I will fight for my happiness, my growth, and my authenticity, knowing that I have the power within me to create the life I desire.

Reclaim the power within by any means necessary. Fight until you can'tfight anymore. Find the center of who you were before losing your way. In doing so, you will discover a strength and resilience that will carry you through life's challenges and lead you to a future filled with hope, fulfillment, and joy.

**Grandma Vernesta's Words of
Wisdom on Encouraging Yourself:**
*"You might be the only person who can speak
an encouraging word to yourself. It's okay; that
might be all you need to keep going."*

Reflect on your Self -Encouragement Journey:

- What accomplishments are you most proud of, and how can you remind yourself of these achievements when you need encouragement?

- Reflect on a time when you supported yourself through a difficult situation. What inner resources did you draw upon, and how can you access them again?

- Write down five positive statements or affirmations that you can use to uplift yourself when you're feeling down. How do these affirmations resonate with your current challenges?

- List three things you're grateful for about yourself and how they contribute to your resilience. How can focusing on gratitude shift your mindset during tough times?

- Identify a personal goal you're working towards. What small steps can you take to motivate yourself, and how will achieving this goal improve your self-confidence?

Good or Bad, You Will Be Influenced, or Someone Will Influence You

Above all else, guard your heart, for everything you do flows from it.

– (PROVERBS 4:23 NIV)

You are not obligated to have relationships with family members who are not good for your mental health. I had to set boundaries. I had what you might consider afflicted compassion, the kind that kept me tethered to unhealthy relationships because I felt a sense of duty and guilt. However, over time, I realized that prioritizing my mental health was crucial for my well-being and growth.

It was often said to me that family was everything. The bond shared with family members was sacred and unbreakable, and it was my duty to maintain these relationships no matter what. This ideology was ingrained in me from a young age, and I took it to heart. However, as I grew older, I began to see the cracks in this idealized notion. Not all family members had my best interests at heart, and some relationships were more harmful than beneficial.

Afflicted compassion was a significant part of my struggle. It was the compassion that compelled me to stay in toxic relationships because I felt sorry for the other person, feared their reaction, or worried about the family dynamics if I set boundaries. This kind of compassion was not healthy; it was rooted in guilt and obligation rather than genuine care and mutual respect.

One of the hardest lessons I had to learn was that compassion does not mean enduring mistreatment or neglecting my own needs. True compassion includes compassion for oneself. It means recognizing when a relationship is damaging and taking the necessary steps to protect one's mental and emotional well-being.

I had a particularly challenging relationship with a close family member who was manipulative and emotionally abusive. Their words and actions left me feeling inadequate, constantly on edge, and questioning my worth. Despite the pain, I kept trying to mend the relationship, believing that it was my responsibility to make it work. I thought things would eventually improve if I just tried harder and was more understanding. But they didn't. The more I gave, the more they took, leaving me drained and emotionally exhausted.

Setting boundaries was not an easy process. It required a great deal of introspection and courage. I had to acknowledge the reality of the situation and accept that some relationships, even those with family, can be detrimental. I had to overcome the internalized guilt and the fear of being judged by others for stepping away from a family member.

The first step in setting boundaries was to define what was acceptable and what was not. I had to be clear about my limits and communicate them firmly. This meant having difficult conversations and being prepared for resistance and backlash. It meant standing my ground even when others didn't understand or support my decision.

I remember the day I finally confronted this family member. My heart was pounding, and my palms were sweaty, but I knew I had to do it. I calmly explained how their behavior affected me and why I needed to distance myself.

As expected, the reaction was not positive. They tried to guilt-trip me, accused me of being selfish, and even attempted to turn other family members against me. But I stood firm. I knew that my mental health was more important than maintaining a facade of a harmonious family relationship.

The aftermath was challenging. I felt a mix of relief and sadness. There were moments of doubt and guilt, wondering if I had made the right decision. However, as time passed, I began to see the positive impact of setting those boundaries. I felt a sense of liberation and empowerment. I was no longer subjected to the constant negativity and manipulation. I had more energy to focus on relationships that were healthy and uplifting.

One of the most significant realizations I had during this process was that I was not alone. Many people struggle with toxic family dynamics and face similar dilemmas. Sharing my experience with friends and a therapist helped me gain perspective and validate my feelings. It reinforced the idea that setting boundaries was not only acceptable but necessary for my well-being.

Over time, I also learned that setting boundaries doesn't always mean cutting ties completely. In some cases, it can mean limiting interactions and maintaining a safe distance. It's about finding a balance that protects your mental health while navigating complex family dynamics.

Through this journey, I developed a stronger sense of self-worth and confidence. I learned to prioritize my needs and well-being without feeling guilty. I also became more compassionate towards myself, understanding that I deserved to be treated with respect and kindness.

Afflicted compassion no longer dictated my actions. I embraced a healthier form of compassion that included caring for myself. I realized that it was possible to love and care for others while also protecting my mental health. This shift in perspective allowed me to cultivate more meaningful and balanced relationships.

In the end, setting boundaries with family members who were not good for my mental health was one of the most empowering decisions I ever made. It allowed me to reclaim my peace and happiness. It taught me the importance of self-care and self-respect. It showed me that I was not obligated to maintain toxic relationships out of a sense of duty or guilt.

Now, I am more mindful of the relationships I invest in. I surround myself with people who uplift and support me, respect my boundaries, and value my well-being. I am no longer afraid to distance myself from harmful relationships, knowing that my mental health comes first.

If you find yourself in a similar situation, remember that you are not alone. It's okay to set boundaries with family members who are not good for your mental health. It's okay to prioritize your well-being and protect your peace. You deserve to be in relationships that are nurturing and respectful. You deserve to be happy.

As you navigate this journey, be kind to yourself. Acknowledge your feelings and give yourself permission to take the necessary steps for your well-being. Seek support from friends, therapists, or support groups. Surround yourself with people who understand and validate your experiences.

Remember, setting boundaries is an act of self-love and self-respect. It's a way of reclaiming your power and taking control of your life. It's about creating a healthy environment where you can thrive and be your authentic self. You have the right to choose the relationships that are good for your mental health, and you are not obligated to maintain those that are not. Through this process, you will discover a stronger, more resilient version of yourself. You will learn to trust your instincts and honor your needs. You will find peace in knowing that you are taking steps to protect your mental health and well-being.

You are not obligated to have relationships with family members who are not good for your mental health. Setting boundaries is essential for your well-being and growth. Afflicted compassion, rooted in guilt and obligation, can keep you tethered to unhealthy relationships. However, true compassion includes compassion for oneself. Prioritizing your mental health and setting boundaries is an act of self-love and self-respect. It's a journey that requires courage and determination, but it leads to a more fulfilling and balanced life. Surround yourself with people who uplift and support you and remember that you deserve to be happy and treated with kindness and respect. Reclaim your power, protect your peace, and embrace the relationships that are good for your mental health.

Grandma Vernesta's Words of Wisdom on Boundaries:
"Once people show you they mean you no good,
feed people out of long-handled spoons."

Reflect on Your Journey Keeping Boundaries:

- 🖎 Reflect on a time when you realized that someone in your life did not have your best interests at heart. How did their actions or words reveal their true intentions? Write about the moment you understood their lack of goodwill and its impact on you.

- 🖎 Consider the importance of setting boundaries with people who mean you no good. Write about specific boundaries you have established or need to establish to protect your well-being. How do these boundaries help you maintain a healthy and positive environment?

- 🖎 Think about the concept of "feeding people out of a long-handled spoon"—keeping a safe distance emotionally. Write about someone you have had to keep at a distance for your own peace of mind. How do you manage this relationship while still being civil and respectful?

- 🖎 Reflect on what you have learned from past experiences with people who did not mean you well. How have these experiences shaped your approach to new relationships and interactions? Write about the lessons learned and how they guide your current actions and decisions.

- 🖎 Write about how maintaining distance from harmful people is an act of self-respect and self-care. How do you prioritize your mental and emotional health in your relationships? Reflect on the benefits of surrounding yourself with supportive and positive individuals.

A Rainy - Day Fund

*Bring the whole tithe into the storehouse,
that there may be food in my house. Test
me in this,' says the LORD Almighty, 'and
see if I will not throw open the floodgates of
heaven and pour out so much blessing that
there will not be room enough to store it.*

– (MALACHI 3:10 NIV)

In my childhood, my grandmother often talked about the emphasis on tithing. She held a deep, unwavering belief in the practice, which she instilled in me from a young age. According to her, tithing was not just a religious obligation but a profound act of faith and stewardship that brought about divine blessings and financial stability. Her teachings on tithing became a cornerstone of my financial habits and played a significant role in shaping my views on money and giving.

My grandmother would recount stories from the Bible, especially those about the Israelites who were instructed to give a tenth of their earnings to God. She would say, "The first fruits of your labor belong to the Lord." These words resonated with me deeply. She emphasized that tithing was an act of gratitude, a way to acknowledge that everything we have is a blessing from God. It was not merely about the money but about trusting in God's provision and being a good steward of His gifts.

As a child, I was curious about how giving away money could lead to more blessings. My grandmother explained it in simple yet profound terms. She said that by tithing, we were sowing seeds into fertile ground. These seeds, she assured me, would grow and bear fruit, ensuring that we would have enough not just for today but for rainy days as well. This concept of sowing and reaping became deeply ingrained in my mind. She made me understand that tithing was a way to invest in God's kingdom, which would yield returns in ways we might not always foresee.

I started practicing tithing with my small allowances and any money I received for birthdays or holidays. Every Sunday, I would set aside a portion of my earnings to take to church. Initially, it felt challenging to part with my hard-earned money, but my grandmother's words would echo in my mind. She often reminded me, "Sowing your tithes ensures that you will have a guaranteed provision." This phrase became a mantra for me. I began to see tithing not as a loss but as a means of securing a brighter, more stable future.

As I grew older, the habit of tithing became second nature. It was no longer a ritual but a deliberate and joyful act of worship. In college, when money was tight, and expenses were high, I continued to tithe faithfully. My grandmother's teachings instilled in me a deep trust that God would provide for my needs. There were times when unexpected expenses arose, but somehow, there was always enough to cover them. I started to see firsthand the truth in my grandmother's words about God's provision.

One particular instance stands out in my memory. During my sophomore year in college, I faced a financial crisis. I had run out of my savings due to my student athletic obligations, and I struggled to make ends meet. I had a car note and everyday expenses to cover. I felt overwhelmed and anxious. Despite my dire financial situation, I continued to tithe. Unexpectedly, I received a $50.00. I remembered my grandmother's assurance that sowing my tithes would ensure a guaranteed provision.

This experience solidified my belief in the power of tithing. It wasn't just about giving money but about exercising faith and trusting in God's promises. My rainy-day fund, which my grandmother had spoken of, was not just a savings account but a spiritual reserve built through acts of generosity and obedience. It was a testament to God's faithfulness and the fruits of sowing seeds in His kingdom.

Over the years, I have encountered numerous other examples of how tithing has brought about unexpected blessings. Whenever I faced financial uncertainty, I found that my needs were met in surprising and often miraculous ways. The habit of tithing taught me discipline and reinforced the importance of putting God first in all aspects of my life, including my finances.

As I transitioned into adulthood and started my career, the principle of tithing continued to guide me. My income increased, and with it, my tithes grew as well. I made it a priority to give the first ten percent of my earnings to my church. It wasn't always easy, especially when there were tempting financial opportunities or pressing expenses. However, I remained steadfast in my commitment, remembering my grandmother's wisdom and the numerous times God had come through for me. I lived in an apartment in Charlotte, NC, and I recall not having any food in the apartment to eat. I also didn't have any money after paying all my bills. I started having a conversation with God and reminded him that he said he would provide all my needs. I decided to go to the grocery store on faith. I picked out bread, deli meat, cereal, and milk. I figured that would provide enough food before payday. I prayed as I was putting those four items in the shopping cart. I got to the register and swiped my debit card, and to my surprise, I had enough money to cover the food.

One of the most significant blessings I received was the ability to buy my first home. It was something I had always dreamed of but seemed out of reach, given the high property prices. However, through consistent tithing and careful financial planning, I was able to save enough for a down payment. When the perfect house came on the market, I was in a position to make an offer. The process went smoothly, and I knew it was another instance of God's provision, made possible through my obedience in tithing.

The habit of tithing has also influenced how I manage my finances. It has taught me to live within my means, prioritize my spending, and save diligently. The concept of sowing and reaping has made me more mindful of where I allocate my resources. I have become more generous, not just in my tithes but in other areas of giving as well. Supporting charitable causes and helping those in need has become a significant part of my life, inspired by the principle of tithing.

Tithing has deepened my faith and trust in God. It has been a tangible way of acknowledging His lordship over my life and finances. Whenever I face financial challenges, I am reminded of His faithfulness and the countless times He has provided for me. Tithing has become an act of worship, a way to honor God and express my gratitude for His blessings.

Grandma Vernesta's wisdom on tithing and saving:
*"Save a little something for a rainy day. If
you make ten dollars, save five dollars. Don't
let money burn a hole in your pocket."*

Reflect on Your Tithing Journey

- How does having a healthy savings account influence your ability to tithe consistently? Reflect on how financial stability through savings enables you to give more freely and generously. How does this connection affect your overall approach to managing money?

- Reflect on a time when having savings allowed you to tithe without financial strain. How did this experience reinforce the importance of both saving and giving? What lessons did you learn from this situation that you can apply to your future financial planning?

- How do you budget for both savings and tithing? Reflect on your budgeting strategies and how you can create a balanced financial plan that prioritizes saving for the future and giving back. What changes can you make to ensure that both areas are adequately funded?

- How does trusting in God's provision influence your approach to savings and tithing? Reflect on the role of faith in your financial decisions and how it helps you balance the need to save with the commitment to tithe. How can you strengthen your trust in God's provision as you manage your finances?

Be True to
Who You Are

*I praise you because I am fearfully
and wonderfully made; your works are
wonderful; I know that full well.*

– (PSALMS 139:14 NIV)

Overcoming imposter syndrome is a journey fraught with challenges and triumphs. It requires a deep understanding of oneself, the ability to differentiate between constructive criticism and projection, and the courage to stay true to your own path. Throughout my life, I have learned that some people are meant to bless you and others to curse you. The tricky part is knowing the difference because both can smile at you. This understanding has been crucial in my journey toward self-acceptance and overcoming imposter syndrome.

Imposter syndrome can be described as a persistent feeling of inadequacy despite evident success. It is the internal dialogue that convinces you that you are a fraud, that you don't deserve your achievements, and that sooner or later, you will be exposed. I have often faced these feelings throughout my career, particularly when stepping into new roles or facing new challenges. It often felt like an internal battle, where the fear of being found out overshadowed my achievements.

The journey to overcoming imposter syndrome begins with acknowledging its presence. For years, I ignored the nagging voice in my head that told me I wasn't good enough. I thought it was just part of being ambitious, but it was more than that. It was a deep-seated insecurity that prevented me from fully embracing my potential. The first step was to recognize that these feelings were not a true reflection of my abilities but a manifestation of my fears and doubts.

One pivotal moment in my journey came during a leadership training session. The facilitator asked us to list our accomplishments and then share them with the group. As I hesitantly recounted my achievements, I realized how significant they were when seen through the eyes of others. Their positive feedback and encouragement helped me see that I was indeed capable and deserving of my success. This exercise was a powerful reminder that our fears can often skew our self-perception, and sometimes, we need others to help us see our true worth.

However, overcoming imposter syndrome isn't just about internal validation. It's also about dealing with external factors, particularly the projections of others. People project their insecurities onto you for various reasons: jealousy, fear, or simply because they are dealing with their own internal battles. Understanding this helped me separate my self-worth from the opinions of others. I realized that not all feedback reflected my abilities. Some of it was a projection of their own insecurities.

Throughout my career, I have encountered individuals who, despite their smiling faces, were not supportive. These people subtly undermined my confidence, often questioning my decisions and capabilities. Initially, their words would sting, causing me to question myself. However, I learned to recognize the difference between constructive criticism and destructive projection over time. Constructive criticism is given with the intention to help you grow, whereas destructive projection is meant to bring you down.

One key lesson I learned is that you have to be at peace with your actions and decisions. This means making choices that align with your values and goals, regardless of what others might say. When I started trusting my instincts and believing in my decisions, I found that I could sleep better at night. I wasn't haunted by the fear of making mistakes or the judgment of others. Instead, I felt a sense of peace knowing that I was true to myself.

This peace is crucial because you may not be everyone's cup of tea, but you still have to sparkle. Not everyone will understand or appreciate your journey, and that's okay. What matters is that you stay true to who you are and continue to shine in your own unique way. Embracing your uniqueness is one of the most empowering steps in overcoming imposter syndrome. It's about recognizing that your differences are your strengths, not weaknesses.

To illustrate, I recall when I was leading a major project at work. The project was high-stakes, and the pressure was immense. As the project progressed, I received mixed feedback from my team and superiors. Some praised my leadership, while others questioned my methods. I found myself slipping back into imposter syndrome, doubting my abilities and fearing failure. During this time, I remembered a piece of advice from a mentor: "Trust your process and believe in your vision. Not everyone will see what you see, and that's okay."

Taking this advice to heart, I focused on the end goal and stayed true to my vision. I made decisions based on my knowledge and experience, even when they were unpopular. The project eventually succeeded, surpassing expectations. It was a reaffirming experience that taught me the importance of trusting myself and not letting others' doubts sway me. I learned that I didn't need everyone's approval to succeed; I just needed to believe in myself.

Another important aspect of overcoming imposter syndrome is surrounding yourself with a supportive network. Having mentors, friends, and colleagues who believe in you can make a significant difference. They can offer perspective, encouragement, and honest feedback. My Grandmother's teachings about discernment in relationships have been invaluable here. She often said, "Some people are meant to bless you, and some are meant to curse you, but you must know the difference because they both are smiling." This wisdom has helped me choose my inner circle wisely, ensuring that I am surrounded by those who uplift and support me. One of the most profound moments in my journey was realizing the power of self-affirmation. Positive affirmations and self-talk can counteract the negative voices of imposter syndrome. I began a daily practice of affirming my worth and capabilities. Statements like "I am competent and capable" and "I deserve my success" became my morning mantra. Over time, these affirmations helped rewire my thinking and build my confidence.

It's also essential to celebrate your successes, no matter how small they might seem. Acknowledging your achievements helps reinforce the belief that you are capable and deserving. I started keeping a journal of my accomplishments, both big and small. Reviewing this journal during moments of doubt has been incredibly empowering. It serves as a tangible reminder of my progress and capabilities.

Furthermore, practicing self-compassion is crucial in this journey. We are often our harshest critics, and imposter syndrome thrives on this self-criticism. Learning to be kind to myself, especially during failures and setbacks, has been transformative. I remind myself that everyone makes mistakes, and these are growth opportunities, not proof of inadequacy.

Another strategy that has helped me is seeking continuous learning and development. The more knowledge and skills I acquire, the more confident I feel in my abilities. This doesn't mean I have to be an expert in everything, but it's about being open to learning and improving. Embracing a growth mindset has helped me view challenges as opportunities rather than threats.

Throughout this journey, I have also come to appreciate the importance of mindfulness and stress management. Practices such as meditation, yoga, and deep-breathing exercises help me stay grounded and focused. They provide a mental reset, allowing me to approach challenges calmly and clearly. Being at peace with my actions and decisions, as my grandmother advised, is easier when I am centered and mindful.

In conclusion, overcoming imposter syndrome is a multifaceted journey that involves self-awareness, resilience, and a strong support system. It requires recognizing the difference between constructive criticism and projection and not allowing others' insecurities to undermine your self-worth. Understanding that some people are meant to bless you and others to curse you, while both may smile at you, is crucial in navigating relationships and maintaining your mental health.

Staying true to your values and decisions, finding peace in your actions, and embracing your uniqueness are key components of this journey. You may not be everyone's cup of tea, but that doesn't mean you should dull your sparkle. Celebrate your successes, practice self-compassion, and continuously seek growth and learning.

You have the power to overcome imposter syndrome and reclaim your confidence. Trust yourself, believe in your worth, and keep shining brightly. You deserve to be at peace with who you are and the path you are on. Let your light shine, and don't let the doubts of others dim your brilliance.

**Grandma Vernesta's Words of
Wisdom on Being True to Yourself:**
*"God made only one you. Greater is he that is in me
than he that is in the world. God gave you the power
to do anything and be anything you want to be."*

Reflect on Your Journey on Being Yourself:

- What are some personal achievements that you are proud of? Reflect on the hard work, dedication, and skills that helped you accomplish these goals. How do these achievements demonstrate your worth and deservingness?

- What are your unique strengths and positive qualities? Reflect on how these traits benefit you and those around you. How do these strengths make you deserving of respect, love, and success?

- Think about a time when you overcame a significant challenge or obstacle. What inner resources did you draw upon to navigate this difficult time? How does overcoming this challenge affirm your worthiness and resilience?

- Recall some instances where you received positive feedback or compliments from others. How did these affirmations make you feel? Reflect on the truth in these positive words and how they highlight your worth and deservingness.

- How can you practice self-compassion and self-love in your daily life? Reflect on ways to be kinder to yourself and acknowledge your worthiness without any conditions. How can self-compassion help you feel more deserving of happiness, success, and love?

CHAPTER

24

Just Go

*A time to search and a time to give up, a
time to keep and a time to throw away.*

— (ECCLESIASTES 3:6 NIV)

Isaiah 43:2 was an anchor for me during the toughest time of my life. The
world was shut down due to COVID-19.

My employer was misogynistic and racist, yet I stayed because I had
become the breadwinner and knew there were many things to get
done. They treated me as if I had no other option but to stay. I should
have known it wasn't the place for me when they didn't want to use my
Historical Black College and University (HBCU) undergraduate alma mater
in the announcement of my arrival. I corrected them a few times, but
they insisted on using a Predominantly White Institution (PWI) instead. The
blatant disrespect didn't stop there. The business decisions I made for my
department were questioned and undermined for no reason. I could have
dealt with it, but I decided that it was time for me to go. I was not going to
be devalued and marginalized any longer. I trusted God for financial cover
and support. I had school tuition, a mortgage, and other responsibilities.
My grandmother had taught me not to stay where I wasn't wanted. So, I
resigned without a job offer in hand.

In the spring of 2020, the world as we knew it changed drastically. The COVID-19 pandemic brought about unprecedented challenges and uncertainties. During this global crisis, I faced personal losses that tested my strength. The death of my grandmother, who had been a pillar of strength and wisdom in my life, was a devastating blow. On top of that, my marriage fell apart, adding to the emotional turmoil. Isaiah says, "When you pass through the waters, I will be with you; and when you pass through the rivers, they will not sweep over you. When you walk through the fire, you will not be burned; the flames will not set you ablaze" (Isaiah 43:2 NIV). This became a source of comfort and strength for me during these dark times.

Compounding my personal grief was the toxicity of my workplace. My employer's blatant misogyny and racism were demoralizing. Despite the oppressive environment, I felt trapped by my financial responsibilities, so I stayed. As the primary breadwinner, I had to ensure that bills were paid, and obligations met. The necessity of my income was a chain that kept me bound to a place that was slowly eroding my self-worth and professional dignity.

There were red flags about the company's culture and values from the outset. One of the earliest signs was their refusal to acknowledge my HBCU (Historically Black Colleges and Universities) undergraduate alma mater in official announcements. This was not merely an oversight but a deliberate decision to replace it with a PWI (Predominantly White Institution). This erasure of my background and the dismissal of the significance of my educational experience were deeply insulting. It was a clear indicator that they did not respect or value the diversity I brought to the table.

The disrespect extended beyond just the issue of my alma mater. My professional decisions and contributions were constantly questioned and undermined. Each business decision I made for my department was scrutinized to the point of being nullified. It felt as though my expertise and judgment were perpetually in doubt, not because of my performance but because of who I was.

The workplace environment was stifling. Colleagues who should have been allies often sided with the leadership's discriminatory practices, either out of fear or complicity. Every day was a battle to maintain my dignity in a place that sought to strip it away. The stress and emotional toll were immense, yet I persisted because I believed I had no other option.

After enduring the relentless disrespect and realizing the detrimental impact it was having on my mental health, I knew I had to make a change. My Grandmother's teachings echoed in my mind – she had always advised against staying where I wasn't wanted or didn't feel valued. Despite the financial risks, I decided to resign. This decision was not made lightly; it was a leap of faith rooted in a deep trust in God's provision and the belief that I deserved better.

Walking away from a steady paycheck with no job offer in hand was terrifying. I had significant financial responsibilities, including school tuition and a mortgage. But the alternative – continuing to work in an environment that devalued and marginalized me – was no longer an option. I trusted God, believing He would guide and support me through this uncertain period.

My Grandmother's legacy was a beacon of guidance. She had faced numerous adversities in her life with grace and strength. Her resilience and wisdom inspired me to persevere. Remembering her words and the values she instilled in me; I found the courage to take control of my destiny and seek an environment where I was respected and valued.

Leaving my toxic job was the first step towards reclaiming my life. The period that followed was challenging, but it was also a time of growth and self-discovery. I took time to reflect on my career goals and what I truly wanted from my professional life. This introspection was crucial in helping me identify the kind of work environment that would allow me to thrive.

I began networking and exploring new opportunities, seeking roles that aligned with my values and aspirations. This period of job searching was not without its difficulties, but I remained steadfast in my belief that God had a plan for me. Each interview and application was an opportunity to showcase my skills and find a place where I could make a meaningful impact.

Eventually, my perseverance paid off. I secured a position at a company that not only valued my professional expertise but also embraced diversity and inclusion. The contrast between my new workplace and my previous employer was stark. Here, I was appreciated for who I was and what I brought to the table. My decisions were respected, and my contributions were recognized. This new role allowed me to grow both professionally and personally. The supportive environment fostered my creativity and innovation, enabling me to excel. The respect and camaraderie I experienced with my new colleagues was refreshing and invigorating. For the first time in a long while, I felt truly valued and fulfilled in my work.

Looking back, I am grateful for the challenges I faced. They tested my faith and resilience, pushing me to stand up for myself and seek better. Isaiah 43:2 remained a pillar of strength throughout this journey, reminding me that I was never alone. The trials I endured have made me stronger and more determined to advocate for myself and others.

My experience has also deepened my commitment to promoting diversity and inclusion in the workplace. I am now more aware of the importance of creating environments where everyone feels respected and valued. This has become a central part of my professional mission, and I strive to be an advocate for positive change wherever I go. Isaiah 43:2 was a beacon of hope and strength during the darkest period of my life.

The global pandemic, personal losses, and a toxic work environment could have overwhelmed me, but my faith and the lessons from my grandmother guided me through. By taking a leap of faith and resigning from a demeaning job, I reclaimed my dignity and found a place where I could truly thrive. This journey has taught me the importance of self-respect, resilience, and trust in God's plan. As I move forward, I carry these lessons with me, am committed to fostering environments of respect and inclusion, and am grateful for the strength that carried me through.

Grandma Vernesta's Words of Wisdom on Letting Go:

*"Don't dwell on the past. Cry, but don't stay
there. Experience your emotions, but don't
let them keep you in the same space."*

Reflect on Your Journey of Letting Go:

- What part of your past is difficult to let go of? Reflect on how this experience has affected your life and what lessons you have learned from it. How can acknowledging these lessons help you move forward?

- Why do you think you are holding on to this particular person, situation, or feeling? Explore the emotions and thoughts that keep you attached. How can understanding these attachments help you take steps to let go?

- Imagine your life without the burden of what you are holding on to. How would letting go improve your well-being and open up new opportunities? Describe the positive changes you envision and how they motivate you to move on.

- What symbolic action or ritual can you create to signify letting go of the past? Reflect on a meaningful way to release this burden, whether through writing a letter, creating art, or another personal ritual. How can this act of letting go help you find closure?

- How can you focus more on the present moment and what you have now? Reflect on the aspects of your current life that bring you joy and fulfillment. How can embracing the present help you release the hold of the past and move forward with a positive outlook?

Standing In Your Truth

Jesus did not let him, but said, 'Go home to your own people and tell them how much the Lord has done for you, and how he has had mercy on you.

— (MARK 5:19 NIV)

I dealt with postpartum depression after having my second child. It was a dark time for me. It took everything in me to get up in the morning and have a normal day. I remember sharing that with someone, and they scolded me for sharing it because people might look at it as if it were a bad thing. I was trying to help someone, yet it was turned into a conversation about me exposing something bad about myself. I am an authentic person and have nothing to hide, so I wondered why I was being encouraged to conceal something that had been a part of who I was. It wasn't hurting them. It was to help them see that you can make it. You can live a beautiful life and thrive.

Dealing with inauthentic people can be dangerous. They live in a world that isn't even their own. I was reminded that you must be cautious about the friendships you make. Either they will influence you, or you will influence them. I did not like this. I was trying to help someone, but they were trying to vilify the situation.

Being a mother at an advanced maternal age, thirty-five and over, brought about unexpected postpartum depression for me. People often dismiss it as mere "baby blues," but it is a real diagnosis. I wanted to open up about my experience, but when I shared it with someone, they scolded me, saying it was taboo to discuss. Many women have had this experience but choose not to talk about it, often hiding their struggles.

However, I didn't see it as a scar. I viewed it as a part of my personal journey. By sharing my story, I hope to help others who may have had similar experiences. Postpartum depression is a significant and often misunderstood challenge, especially for older mothers. It's essential to recognize and address it openly. Talking about it not only helps to normalize the experience but also provides support and validation to those who might be suffering in silence.

The stigma surrounding mental health, especially postpartum depression, is pervasive and damaging. Many people still view mental health struggles as a sign of weakness or something to be ashamed of. This stigma prevents many from seeking the help they need and contributes to the isolation and suffering of those affected. By sharing my story, I hoped to break through that stigma and show others that it's okay to struggle and it's okay to seek help.

Despite the criticism, I remained committed to being open about my experiences. Authenticity is a core value of mine, and I believe that being true to oneself is essential for personal growth and fulfillment. My postpartum depression was a part of my life, and it shaped me in significant ways. Denying or hiding it would have been a disservice to myself and others who might benefit from hearing my story.

I also wanted to help others by sharing my journey. Postpartum depression is more common than many realize, especially for women who are of advanced maternal age, and it's crucial for those going through it to know that they are not alone. By being candid about my struggles, I hoped to offer support and encouragement to others facing similar challenges. My goal was to show that you can overcome even the darkest times and go on to live a beautiful, thriving life.

I am grateful for the strength and wisdom I gained from my experiences, and I am committed to helping others who are going through similar challenges. By sharing my story and being open about my struggles, I hope to inspire and support others to seek help, embrace their authenticity, and believe in their ability to overcome and thrive.

**Grandma Vernesta's Words of
Wisdom on Sharing Your Journey:**
*"Don't be afraid to share your testimony.
Sharing your testimony can help someone
through their struggles and trust God."*

Reflect on Your Journey of Transparency:

🖋 Reflect on a specific moment in your life when you felt God's presence and help the most. Describe the situation, how you felt then, and how God's intervention made a difference. How did this experience strengthen your faith?

🖋 How has your relationship with God transformed you personally? Reflect on the changes in your character, mindset, and behavior since you started relying on God's guidance. How can you share this transformation with others to inspire and encourage them?

🖋 Think about the everyday ways in which God helps and blesses you. Reflect on the small, often overlooked blessings and how they impact your daily life. How can acknowledging these blessings enhance your gratitude and faith?

🖋 Describe a significant challenge or hardship you faced and how your faith helped you overcome it. Reflect on the prayers, scriptures, or spiritual practices that provided comfort and guidance. How can you share this testimony to offer hope to others going through similar struggles?

🖋 What are your hopes and aspirations for the future, and how do you seek God's guidance in pursuing them? Reflect on how you trust in God's plan and the steps you take to align your goals with His will. How can sharing your faith journey inspire others to trust in God's guidance for their own lives?

CHAPTER 26

Keep a Low Profile and Maintain Peace

But avoid foolish controversies and genealogies and arguments and quarrels about the law, because these are unprofitable and useless. Warn a divisive person once, and then warn them a second time. After that, have nothing to do with them. You may be sure that such people are warped and sinful; they are self-condemned.

— (TITUS 3:9-11 NIV)

Although I was taught to keep the peace in situations, it was often at my expense. I often heard the value of maintaining harmony was emphasized repeatedly. Conflict was seen as something to be avoided at all costs, and I internalized this lesson deeply. However, the cost of this peacekeeping was personal and significant. I learned to be a doormat and was often taken advantage of. I would allow people to say things that hurt but not address them. Who was I keeping the peace for? Certainly not me. I began to resent keeping the peace because it often left me upset and angry. There was a difference between addressing ignorance and just allowing someone to be disrespectful. Instead of dealing with ignorance, I would rather remove myself from the situation.

From a young age, I was taught that peacekeeping was paramount. My family valued harmony above all else, and any form of conflict was quickly suppressed. This upbringing instilled in me a strong desire to avoid confrontation. The message was clear: keeping the peace was synonymous with being a good, considerate person.

At school and in social situations, I carried this lesson with me. Whenever conflicts arose, I would step back, avoid taking sides, and do my best to smooth things over. While this often diffused tension in the short term, it also meant that my own feelings and needs were frequently overlooked. I became adept at swallowing my grievances, prioritizing others' comfort over mine.

As I grew older, the personal cost of this peacekeeping approach became more apparent. In high school, I found myself in friendships where I was routinely taken advantage of. I was the one who always compromised, always gave in, and always went the extra mile to maintain harmony. My friends knew they could rely on me to keep things calm, but this often meant they pushed my boundaries, sometimes knowingly, sometimes not.

One incident stands out in particular. A close friend made a series of hurtful remarks about my appearance in front of others. It stung deeply, but instead of confronting her, I laughed it off, trying to keep the atmosphere light. I felt humiliated and betrayed inside, but I convinced myself that addressing it would create unnecessary conflict. This pattern repeated itself numerous times with different people in different situations. Each time, my self-esteem took another hit.

The turning point came during my first job after college. I worked in a small office where the culture was informal and friendly on the surface, but underneath, it was rife with passive-aggressive behavior and backhanded comments. My supervisor had a knack for making cutting remarks under the guise of humor. Initially, I tried to laugh along, not wanting to disrupt the peace.

However, the constant undermining and subtle insults wore me down as time went on. I started to dread going to work, feeling anxious and devalued. One day, after a particularly harsh comment, I realized that keeping the peace was taking a significant toll on my mental health. I was sacrificing my well-being for the sake of avoiding conflict, and it was no longer sustainable.

Recognizing the need for change, I began to explore ways to assert myself without sacrificing my values. I read books on communication and conflict resolution, attended workshops, and sought advice from mentors. Slowly, I started to practice setting boundaries and addressing issues directly but calmly. One of the first times I put this into practice was during a team meeting. My supervisor made a snide remark about my recent project, implying it was subpar. Instead of laughing it off or staying silent, I took a deep breath and responded assertively. I calmly explained the rationale behind my decisions and highlighted the positive feedback the project had received from our clients. The room fell silent momentarily, and then the conversation moved on.

To my surprise, there was no explosion of conflict, just a recognition of my perspective. This experience was empowering. It showed me that it was possible to stand up for myself without creating chaos. Over time, I became more comfortable with assertiveness. I learned to address disrespectful behavior and set clear boundaries, which significantly improved my self-esteem and overall well-being.

One of the crucial lessons I learned during this period was the difference between addressing ignorance and allowing disrespect. Ignorance often stems from a lack of knowledge or understanding. It can usually be addressed through calm, informative conversations. Disrespect, on the other hand, is a deliberate disregard for another person's feelings or boundaries.

Addressing my tendency to keep the peace at my own expense had a significant positive impact on my mental health. As I became more assertive and established healthier boundaries, my anxiety levels decreased, and my overall sense of well-being improved. I no longer carried the constant burden of unaddressed grievances and unspoken frustrations. One of the most rewarding aspects of this transformation has been the ability to inspire others. By sharing my journey and modeling assertiveness, I have been able to support friends and colleagues who struggle with similar issues. I encourage them to prioritize their own well-being and to recognize the importance of self-respect in their interactions.

There comes a point in life when we must recognize that the opinions and actions of others do not define our worth or our path. It's a lesson learned through hardship and resilience: let them not appreciate you, let them be upset, let them judge you, let them misunderstand you, let them gossip about you, let them ignore you, let them be "right," let them doubt you, let them not like you, let them not speak to you, let them run your name in the ground, let them make you out to be the villain. Let them watch God elevate you! Whatever it is that people want to say about you, let them! Kindly step aside and LET THEM.

**Grandma Vernesta's Words of
Wisdom for Keeping the Peace:**

*" You don't always have to address a negative
situation. Lay low and let God take care of it. If you
live long enough, you'll understand by and by."*

Reflect on Your Peacekeeping Journey:

- 🖋 Think about a recent conflict or disagreement you had. What triggered the conflict, and how did you respond? Reflect on what you could have done differently to keep the peace. How can you apply these insights to future interactions?

- 🖋 Recall a situation where you successfully practiced empathy and maintained peace. What steps did you take to understand the other person's perspective? Reflect on how practicing empathy can help you in future interactions and identify ways to enhance your empathy skills.

- 🖋 How do stress and emotions affect your interactions with others? Reflect on specific instances where stress or strong emotions led to conflict. What strategies can you use to manage your emotions better and maintain peace in your interactions?

- 🖋 What communication techniques have you found helpful in keeping the peace? Reflect on the importance of active listening, assertiveness, and clarity in your conversations. How can you improve your communication skills to foster more peaceful interactions?

- 🖋 How can you contribute to creating a peaceful environment in your home, workplace, or community? Reflect on actions you can take to promote harmony and reduce tension. What habits or practices can you adopt to consistently nurture peace in your surroundings?

chapter 27

Don't Dim Your Light

*In the same way, let your light shine before
others, that they may see your good deeds
and glorify your Father in heaven.*

– (MATTHEW 5:16 NIV)

"Don't dim your light for anyone." This belief has guided me through many of life's experiences. We live in a world where insecurities and jealousy often overshadow genuine joy and celebration for others. But it is crucial to remember that each one of us has unique qualities and talents gifted by God. These blessings come to us at the exact time He deems perfect. When we dim our light to make others feel comfortable, we essentially tell God, "Not now; my friend isn't ready yet." This narrative explores the importance of embracing our gifts, celebrating our successes, and not allowing anyone else's insecurities to cause us to question ourselves.

From a young age, I was taught the value of humility and modesty. While these traits are important, they often come with the unspoken rule of not shining too brightly and not standing out too much. As I grew older, I began to understand the difference between humility and self-suppression. Humility acknowledges our strengths and accomplishments without arrogance, while self-suppression hides our light to make others feel more comfortable.

"Don't dim your light for anyone." These words resonated deeply with me, especially when I felt the need to downplay my achievements. Whether it was in school, at work, or in social circles, there were always those who seemed uncomfortable with my success. Their insecurities often manifested as criticism, jealousy, or attempts to belittle my accomplishments. During these moments, I had to remind myself that God has gifted us with unique qualities and talents for a reason. Each of us is meant to shine in our own way.

Insecurities can be incredibly powerful and damaging, not just to those who harbor them but also to those around them. When someone is insecure, they might project their fears and doubts onto others. This projection can cause us to question ourselves, doubt our abilities, and, ultimately, dim our light.

I recall a time in my career when I received a significant promotion. It was a moment of great joy and validation for all my hard work. However, not everyone shared my happiness. A colleague, who I considered a friend, reacted with indifference and subtle negativity. Their behavior made me question whether I should celebrate my success openly. I began to downplay my achievements, not wanting to make them feel uncomfortable or less than.

It was during this period of self-doubt that I realized the importance of not allowing someone else's insecurities to dictate my actions. God has blessed each of us with unique gifts and talents, and it is not our responsibility to make others feel better about themselves by dimming our light. Instead, we should strive to inspire and uplift others, encouraging them to find and embrace their own light.

Celebrating success is an essential part of personal growth and fulfillment. Achieving something significant is a testament to our hard work, dedication, and God's blessings. By celebrating our accomplishments, we acknowledge the journey we have undertaken and the obstacles we have overcome.

However, celebrating success can sometimes be met with resistance from those around us. People who are not genuinely happy for us might expect us to dim our light to avoid making them feel inadequate. This expectation is not only unfair but also detrimental to our self-esteem and growth.

If someone were truly happy for you, they would celebrate you and not expect you to dim your light. Genuine friends and supporters will cheer for your successes and encourage you to shine even brighter. They understand that your success does not diminish their own potential for achievement. Instead of dimming your light, seek out those who celebrate you wholeheartedly and reciprocate that support.

One of the most comforting aspects of faith is the belief that God's timing is perfect. He blesses us with unique qualities and talents at the exact moments we need them. When we question our blessings or feel the need to hide them, we are essentially doubting God's plan for us.

In my own life, there have been instances where I felt unworthy of the blessings I received. I questioned why I was given certain opportunities or talents when others around me seemed more deserving. However, through prayer and reflection, I came to understand that God's timing and wisdom are beyond my comprehension. Each blessing is part of a larger plan, and it is my responsibility to honor and utilize these gifts to the fullest.

Overcoming the pressure to dim your light requires a strong sense of self and a commitment to honoring your gifts.

One of the most rewarding aspects of embracing your light is the ability to inspire others to do the same. By celebrating your success and using your gifts to uplift those around you, you create a ripple effect of positivity and empowerment.

In my own journey, I have found immense joy in mentoring and supporting others. Sharing my experiences and lessons learned has helped others recognize their own potential and embrace their unique gifts. When we shine our light, we not only fulfill our own purpose but also encourage others to find and embrace their own.

Encouraging others to celebrate their achievements and not dim their light is a powerful way to create a supportive and uplifting community. Genuine support and celebration of others' successes foster an environment where everyone can thrive and grow.

"Don't dim your light for anyone." These words are a powerful reminder of the importance of embracing our unique qualities and talents and not allowing others' insecurities to cause us to question ourselves. God has gifted each of us with unique blessings, and it is our responsibility to honor and utilize these gifts to their fullest.

Celebrating our success and not dimming our light is a testament to our hard work, dedication, and faith in God's perfect timing. By surrounding ourselves with genuine supporters, practicing self-reflection and gratitude, and trusting in God's plan, we can overcome the pressure to hide our light and inspire others to do the same.

Remember, if someone were truly happy for you, they would celebrate you and not expect you to dim your light. Embrace your gifts, celebrate your achievements, and let your light shine brightly for all to see. Your light reflects God's blessings, and it is meant to shine at the exact moments He has planned for you.

**Grandma Vernesta's Words of Wisdom
on Operating in your Gift**:
*"God gave you the gift for a reason. Use
your gift, or you will lose it."*

Reflect on Your Journey for Acknowledging Your God-Given Gifts:

- 🖋 What are your unique talents, skills, and qualities that make you special? Reflect on how these attributes positively impact those around you. How can you use these gifts more intentionally to let your light shine in your daily life?

- 🖋 Acknowledging Your Strengths: List five of your greatest strengths and how they have positively impacted on your life and those around you.

- 🖋 Think about a time when you inspired or positively influenced someone else. What did you do, and how did it affect the other person? Reflect on how sharing your light can inspire and uplift others and identify ways to continue doing so.

- 🖋 What does living authentically mean to you? Reflect on how being true to yourself allows your light to shine more brightly. What actions or changes can you make to live more authentically and align with your true self?

- 🖋 What self-doubts or fears hold you back from fully expressing your light? Reflect on specific instances where self-doubt has dimmed your shine. How can you challenge these doubts and take steps to build confidence in your abilities and worth?

God Will Grant You Uncommon Favor

In him we were also chosen, having been predestined according to the plan of him who works out everything in conformity with the purpose of his will.

– (EPHESIANS 1:11 NIV)

In life, we often encounter people who try to cap our potential based on their own limited capacity. They impose their limitations on us, not because we are incapable, but because they cannot fathom managing what we do. Over the years, I have lost count of the times the same people would say to me, "You have a lot going on." Initially, I ignored these comments, but eventually, I began to respond with, "No more than you do." This response was not intended to undermine their abilities but to highlight the unfairness of capping others' capacities based on personal limitations. This chapter explores the concept of "uncommon favor," how it influences perceptions and the importance of self-awareness and authenticity in the face of societal expectations. People will try to cap you at their capacity, often projecting their insecurities and limitations onto you. This phenomenon is not uncommon in both personal and professional settings. When individuals cannot understand how you manage multiple responsibilities or excel in various areas, they might resort to belittling your efforts or questioning your capabilities.

I wasn't saying that to anyone, so why were the same people saying it to me? This question often crossed my mind. It became apparent that these individuals were projecting their insecurities onto me, perhaps feeling threatened or inadequate by comparison. Instead of recognizing and celebrating our differences, they sought to bring me down to their comfort level.

Uncommon favor is a term that resonates deeply with me. It refers to the blessings and opportunities that come to us through divine intervention, often leaving others puzzled about how we manage so much. Uncommon favor causes people to question and wonder about how you are managing. This favor often leads to comments and questions from those who cannot comprehend how you handle your responsibilities.

This interaction highlighted a common societal expectation that one's identity and activities are closely tied to their relationship status. For many, marriage is seen as a defining aspect of one's life, dictating what one can or cannot do. However, this is a narrow and limiting view. Our identities are multifaceted and shaped by our passions, interests, and individual journeys, not merely by marital status.

Self-awareness and authenticity are crucial in navigating societal expectations and judgments and being self-aware means understanding your strengths, weaknesses, and values. It involves recognizing what drives you and what you are passionate about. Conversely, authenticity is about staying true to yourself, regardless of external pressures or expectations.

For me, embracing self-awareness and authenticity meant acknowledging my capabilities and pursuing my passions, even when others doubted or questioned me. It meant standing firm in my identity and not allowing others' perceptions to dictate my actions. When people tried to cap my capacity or define me by their standards, I remained steadfast in my journey, guided by my self-awareness and faith in God's plan.

When faced with doubts and misconceptions from others, it is essential to respond with grace and confidence. When people question your abilities or choices, take the opportunity to clarify your intentions and motivations. Explain your perspective and the reasons behind your actions. Establish boundaries with those who consistently project their insecurities onto you. Communicate your need for support and understanding, and distance yourself from toxic relationships if necessary.

Trust in God's plan and the blessings of uncommon favor. When you feel overwhelmed by others' doubts, turn to prayer and reflection for guidance and strength. Do not shy away from celebrating your achievements. Recognize your hard work and the divine favor that has brought you success and share your joy with those who genuinely support you. Surround yourself with individuals who uplift and encourage you. Seek out mentors, friends, and colleagues who believe in your potential and celebrate your successes.

Overcoming external pressures requires a strong sense of self and a commitment to staying true to your values and beliefs. Be kind to yourself and acknowledge your achievements and efforts. Self-compassion will help you stay motivated and confident, even when faced with criticism. Regularly reflect on your experiences and growth. Self-reflection will help you stay aligned with your values and recognize the progress you have made. Take charge of your narrative and empower yourself to pursue your goals. Do not let others' doubts or limitations define your path. Have faith in God's timing and the blessings of uncommon favor. Trust that you are on the right path and that everything will fall into place at the right moment.

By embracing our own capacity and recognizing the power of uncommon favor, we can inspire others to do the same. When we live authentically and celebrate our successes, we create a ripple effect of positivity and empowerment. Share your journey and experiences with others. Your story can serve as a source of inspiration and encouragement for those facing similar challenges. Offer support and encouragement to those around you. Help them recognize their own potential and embrace their unique gifts. Lead by example and demonstrate the power of living authentically. Show others that it is possible to achieve success without compromising your values or succumbing to external pressures. Foster a community of support and celebration. Surround yourself with like-minded individuals who uplift and encourage each other.

Grandma Vernesta's Words of Wisdom on Favor:

"God will make a way out of no way for you."

Reflect on Your Journey for God's Favor:

- Think about a specific moment when you experienced what you believe to be an uncommon spiritual favor. Describe the situation in detail and reflect on how this favor manifested. How did this experience impact your faith and perspective on divine blessings?

- Reflect on your beliefs about the source of uncommon spiritual favor. What do you attribute these extraordinary blessings to? How does understanding the source of this favor deepen your spiritual journey and relationship with the divine?

- List some uncommon blessings or favors you have received that stand out to you. Reflect on the significance of each one and express your gratitude for these unique experiences. How does recognizing and appreciating these blessings enhance your sense of spiritual connection and gratitude?

- How can you share your experiences of uncommon spiritual favor with others to inspire and uplift them? Reflect on the impact your testimony can have on those who hear it. What specific stories or examples can you share to illustrate the power of divine favor in your life?

- How can you cultivate an attitude of expectation for uncommon spiritual favor in your daily life? Reflect on ways to remain open and receptive to divine blessings, even in ordinary circumstances. How does living with this mindset influence your actions, decisions, and outlook on life?

Speak in the Affirmative

Keep a clear conscience, so that those who speak maliciously against your good behavior in Christ may be ashamed of their slander.

– (1 PETER 3:16 NIV)

Words are powerful. They shape our reality, define our relationships, and build our credibility. Yet, many people fail to recognize the impact of their words, often undermining themselves with a simple conjunction: "but." Saying "but" erases everything you said before that. It nullifies your statements and intentions, casting doubt on your sincerity. My Grandmother always reminded us to let our "nays" be nays and our "yays" be yays. Your word must be impeccable. This principle has guided me through life, emphasizing the importance of integrity, authenticity, and consistency in both speech and action. One of the most common ways we undermine ourselves is by using the word "but" to contradict our own statements. For instance, consider the phrase, "I think you're doing a great job, but..." The "but" instantly negates the praise, leaving the listener focused on the criticism that follows. This pattern not only diminishes the positive impact of our words but also erodes trust and credibility.

I recall a time in my career when a colleague consistently promised to deliver work on time but rarely followed through. Despite their good intentions, the repeated failures to meet deadlines resulted in frustration and mistrust among the team. This experience underscored the importance of aligning actions with words and the negative impact of failing to do so

Your word must be impeccable. This means speaking with integrity, avoiding gossip, and refraining from making promises you cannot keep. It involves communicating clearly and honestly, ensuring that your words reflect your true intentions and values.

Living by this principle requires mindfulness and a commitment to self-awareness. It means taking the time to think before speaking, considering the impact of your words, and being willing to stand by what you say. This level of integrity fosters respect and admiration from others, as they come to see you as a person of principle and reliability. Trust is the cornerstone of any meaningful relationship, whether personal or professional. Building trust requires consistent behavior and communication over time. When people see that your actions consistently match your words, they develop confidence in your reliability and integrity.

In my life, I have found that the most trusted relationships are those with a clear alignment between words and actions. Whether it is fulfilling a promise to a friend or meeting a deadline at work, these consistent behaviors build a reputation of dependability and trustworthiness. Maintaining integrity in our words and actions is not always easy. We face numerous challenges and temptations that can lead us astray. Fear, pressure, and the desire to please others can sometimes cause us to compromise our principles. However, overcoming these challenges is crucial to living a life of authenticity and honor.

Living with integrity and ensuring that our words and actions align requires conscious effort and discipline. Take a moment to consider the impact of your words before you speak. Ensure that your statements are truthful and that you can follow through on any commitments you make. Practice making affirmative statements without undermining them with "but." Instead of saying, "I appreciate your work, but..." try, "I appreciate your work. I also think we can improve on...." Be honest about what you can and cannot do. Setting realistic expectations helps prevent over-promising and under-delivering.

Make it a habit to follow through on your commitments. If you promise something, make every effort to deliver on that promise. If you fall short, take responsibility and communicate openly about what happened. Apologize sincerely and outline steps to prevent recurrence. Regularly reflect on your core values and ensure that your actions align with them. This self-awareness helps maintain integrity even under pressure.

Integrity in words and actions has a profound impact on our relationships. It fosters trust, respect, and a sense of security. When people know they can rely on your word, they feel more connected and valued, strengthening both personal and professional bonds.

In my relationships, I have noticed that those built on a foundation of integrity are the most resilient. They withstand misunderstandings and conflicts because there is a mutual understanding that each party will act honestly and respectfully. This foundation allows for open communication and a deeper level of connection.

Integrity is also a critical component of effective leadership. Leaders who consistently align their actions with their words inspire trust and loyalty in their teams. They set a positive example and create a culture of accountability and honesty.

In my experience as a leader, I have found that demonstrating integrity fosters a positive work environment. When team members see that their leader is reliable and truthful, they are more likely to emulate these behaviors. This creates a cohesive and motivated team that works together towards common goals.

The power of words and the importance of aligning them with our actions cannot be overstated. Saying "but" erases everything you said before that, undermining our communication and credibility. It matters that your actions match your words. When they don't, people question you, and you lose your credibility. My Grandmother's wisdom to let our "nays" be nays and our "yays" be yays is a timeless reminder that our word must be impeccable.

Living with integrity requires mindfulness, self-awareness, and a commitment to honesty. By ensuring that our words and actions align, we build trust, foster meaningful relationships, and create a positive impact in our personal and professional lives. Let us strive to mean what we say, say what we mean, and live each day with authenticity and integrity.

Grandma Vernesta's Words of Wisdom about Integrity:
"Your word and your name are all you have. Do what you say and say what you mean. A lie doesn't care who tells it. If you will lie, you'll steal; if you'll steal, you will kill."

Reflect on Your Journey to Integrity:

- What does integrity mean to you personally? Reflect on your understanding of integrity and why it is important in your life. How do you strive to live with integrity in your daily actions and decisions?

- Think about a recent decision or action you took that aligned with your values and integrity. Describe the situation and how it made you feel. How does this reinforce the importance of keeping a clear conscience in future decisions?

- Recall a time when you faced a moral dilemma. How did you navigate the situation, and what choices did you make? Reflect on what you learned from this experience about maintaining integrity and keeping a clear conscience.

- How do honesty and transparency play a role in maintaining your integrity? Reflect on ways you can be more honest and transparent in your interactions with others. How does practicing these qualities help you maintain a clear conscience?

- How do you ensure that your personal and professional actions align with your values and integrity? Reflect on any challenges you face in maintaining this balance and identify strategies to overcome them. How does living with integrity in all areas of your life contribute to a sense of inner peace and fulfillment?

CHAPTER

30

Hold to God's Unchanging Hands

I give them eternal life, and they shall never perish; no one will snatch them out of my hand. My Father, who has given them to me, is greater than all; no one can snatch them out of my Father's hand.

– (JOHN 10:28-29 NIV)

The 91st Psalm was one of the first chapters in the Bible that my grandmother told me to read. It highlights God's protection in our lives. I committed this chapter to memory and recited it daily. I would sleep with the scripture under my pillow while in college. This scripture guided me and gave me a sense of security when I didn't feel I had any. It created a sense of comfort and confidence in knowing I was protected by God's word.

In life, the only constant is change. Seasons shift, relationships evolve, and circumstances transform, often leaving us feeling unmoored and adrift. Yet, amidst the ceaseless ebb and flow, there is a steadfast anchor: God's unchanging hands. The hymn "Hold to God's Unchanging Hand" has always been one of my absolute favorite songs. Its message resonates deeply, reminding me that despite the world's turbulence, God's constancy offers solace and strength.

Everything around us is in a state of flux, from the mundane to the monumental. Yet, within this song lies a powerful reminder: while earthly things may falter, God's eternal nature remains unchanged. This realization has been a source of comfort and inspiration for me during the most tumultuous times.

Everyone and everything around me were changing. There were times when I felt like I was out in the middle of the ocean with nothing to grasp onto. My job, my marriage, betrayal from friends and family—you name it, it was happening. Each new challenge seemed to compound the uncertainty, leaving me to navigate an overwhelming sea of change.

In my career, I encountered significant instability. Job roles shifted, management changed, and the workplace environment became increasingly unpredictable. This professional upheaval left me feeling insecure and uncertain about my future. Amidst this storm, I clung to the hymn that began with "Trust in Him, who will not leave you."

These words became my lifeline. I sang this song through tears and later through triumph. When everything else was uncertain, the promise of God's unwavering presence provided a sense of stability and hope. Trusting in Him, who does not change, no matter what the years bring, gave me the strength to persevere.

Holding onto God's unchanging hand is not just about seeking comfort but finding the strength to persevere. When you trust in Him, who will not leave you, it empowers you to face life's challenges with courage and resilience. This faith acts as a buffer against the disappointments and betrayals that inevitably come our way.

When earthly friends forsake you, still more closely to Him cling. These moments of isolation and betrayal are incredibly painful, but they also serve as a powerful reminder of where our true source of strength lies. Human relationships are fragile and prone to failure, but God's love and support are constant and unwavering.

I sang this song through tears, finding peace in its message during my darkest hours. The act of singing itself became a form of prayer, a way to communicate my fears, hopes, and faith to God. The tears were a release of the pent-up emotions, a way to cleanse the soul and make space for healing and renewal.

Later, I sang this song through triumph. As I navigated through the storm, I began to see the light on the horizon. The trials and tribulations did not vanish overnight, but I found strength and resilience that I did not know I possessed. This song, once a cry for help, became an anthem of victory. It reminded me of the journey I had undertaken and the divine support that had guided me through it.

"Build your hopes on things eternal" is a call to shift our focus from the transient to the everlasting. Earthly possessions, status, and even relationships are subject to change and decay. By anchoring our hopes and dreams in the eternal, we find a stable foundation that withstands the test of time.

This perspective shift was crucial for me. Instead of fixating on the losses and changes around me, I started to focus on my spiritual growth and the eternal truths that guided my life. This shift in focus brought a sense of peace and purpose, helping me to navigate the changes with grace and confidence.

Life's transitions can be daunting, but they also offer opportunities for growth and renewal. By holding onto God's unchanging hand, we can embrace these changes with faith and optimism. Trusting in God's plan, even when it is not clear to us, allows us to move forward with confidence.

My journey has been one of learning to trust in God's unchanging hands amidst life's swift transitions. It has been about finding stability in the midst of chaos, strength in the face of adversity, and hope in times of despair. This journey is ongoing, but the lessons learned, and the faith gained are invaluable.

While personal faith is crucial, the support of a faith community can provide additional strength and encouragement. During my difficult times, I found solace and support in my church community. Their prayers, encouragement, and shared faith helped bolster my own.

In moments of weakness, the collective strength of my community lifted me up. They reminded me of God's promises and helped me see the light when all seemed dark. This communal support was a testament to the power of shared faith and the importance of surrounding oneself with a supportive and loving community.

Looking back, I see how each trial and tribulation was a step in my journey of faith. The job uncertainties, marital challenges, and betrayals from friends and family were opportunities for growth and deeper reliance on God. Each step, no matter how painful, brought me closer to understanding the true meaning of holding onto God's unchanging hand.

This journey has also reminded me that faith does not eliminate challenges but provides the strength to overcome them. It is a continuous process of learning, growing, and trusting in God's eternal presence and unwavering support.

The lessons learned and the strength gained from holding onto God's unchanging hand are not just for me. They are meant to be shared. By sharing my story and the comfort I found in this hymn, I hope to inspire others who may be going through similar struggles. The message of God's constancy and unwavering support is universal and timeless.

If you are facing swift transitions and feel adrift, remember the power of holding onto God's unchanging hand. Trust in Him who will not leave you, no matter what the years may bring. When your earthly friends forsake you, cling more closely to Him. Build your hopes on things eternal and find strength in the divine constancy that transcends all earthly changes.

By embracing this message, we can navigate life's changes with grace and confidence. We can find stability in the midst of chaos, strength in adversity, and hope in despair. Let us hold onto God's unchanging hand, build our hopes on things eternal, and trust in the unwavering support of the divine. In doing so, we not only find peace and strength for ourselves but also inspire and uplift those around us.

Grandma Vernesta's Words of Wisdom
on Holding on to God's Unchanging Hand:
"The Lord will Never Leave You, Nor Forsake You."

Reflect on Your Journey of Staying Close to God:

- Reflect on a time in your life when you felt God's unwavering support and presence. Describe the situation and how holding on to God's unchanging hand helped you navigate through it. How did this experience strengthen your faith?

- What does trusting in God's plan mean to you? Reflect on how you can maintain trust in God's unchanging hand, even when circumstances are uncertain or challenging. How can this trust guide your decisions and actions?

- Identify and reflect on scriptures that emphasize God's unchanging nature and steadfast love. How do these verses inspire and comfort you? Write about how you can apply these scriptures to your daily life to reinforce your faith and reliance on God.

- Reflect on your prayer life and how it helps you stay connected to God's unchanging hand. Describe a time when prayer provided you with clarity, comfort, or strength. How can you cultivate a more consistent and meaningful prayer practice to deepen your reliance on God?

- How does holding on to God's unchanging hand influence how you approach life's challenges and opportunities? Reflect on how this faith gives you confidence and peace.

- How can you embody this faith in your daily interactions and decisions, inspiring others to also trust in God's steadfastness?

The Final Lesson: You Are a Work in Progress

*Trust in the LORD with all your heart and
lean not on your own understanding;
in all your ways submit to him, and
he will make your paths straight.*

— (PROVERBS 3:5-6 NIV)

Please be patient with me. God is not through with me yet. This phrase resonates deeply with me as I reflect on my life's journey. I have come to understand that God is still writing my story, and I need to stop trying to steal the pen and trust Him completely. Whew! It took me a while to grasp that my life purpose would not be accomplished in a day. My life is a testimony carefully crafted by God, and I am learning to embrace His timing and His plan.

One of the pivotal moments in my journey came after I completed my undergraduate studies. I had just run my last track meet and was eagerly planning my next steps. I received an offer to work for IBM and relocate to Raleigh, NC. With an apartment lined up and plans to move in August, everything seemed to be falling into place. However, life took an unexpected turn when the company rescinded my offer letter due to significant organizational changes. I was devastated. How could I have a four-year degree and no job?

The situation became even more disheartening when a family member who had neither a degree nor a high school diploma asked me how I felt about attending college and still being unemployed. What kind of question was that? It felt like salt in the wound. I knew I had to do something. I needed a plan B, and fast. This experience was one of my first in seeing God orchestrate His plan for my career journey.

During my disappointment, I clung to my faith, trusting that God had a plan even if I couldn't see it yet. After some searching, I found a job and relocated to Charlotte, NC. I worked for six months at an insurance company, but I wanted more. My undergraduate degree was in Marketing, and a colleague informed me that Charlotte Mecklenburg Schools were hiring. Taking a chance, I applied and was hired on the spot to teach Marketing classes to high school students.

Teaching was rewarding, but I still felt that there was something more for me. I signed on with a temporary agency during my summer break and began working at First Union National Bank. On the first day of my temporary assignment, the manager asked if I was seeking full-time employment. My response was cautious: "It depends." I didn't want to leave education, but something was nudging me to be open to new possibilities. By the end of my three-day temporary assignment, I was offered a full-time position as a payroll specialist.

Reflecting on these moments now, I see how they were steppingstones leading to my current role as a C-Suite executive in Human Resources. My initial career goal was to work in the sports arena, but God had a different plan—one that was far better than I could have imagined.

These experiences taught me to trust God's timing and plan. Each setback and redirection was a part of His grand design for my life. It wasn't always easy to understand or accept at the time, but looking back, I see His hand guiding me every step of the way.

Life has a way of throwing curveballs, and it's in those moments of uncertainty and challenge that our faith is tested and strengthened. When I was left without a job offer after graduation, I could have given in to despair. Instead, I trusted that God was not through with me yet. He was still writing my story, and I needed to be patient and let Him lead.

In my professional journey, I have encountered numerous situations that tested my faith and resilience. Each time, I reminded myself that God's plan is perfect and that He is in control. When doors closed, it wasn't the end—it was merely a redirection toward something greater that He had in store for me.

My time in education was immensely fulfilling. Teaching Marketing to high school students allowed me to share my knowledge and passion with the next generation. Yet, there was a part of me that yearned for something more. When the opportunity at First Union National Bank presented itself, I felt a mix of excitement and hesitation. Could this be the next step in God's plan for me?

Accepting the full-time position as a payroll specialist was a leap of faith. It was a significant change from teaching, but I felt a sense of peace and assurance that this was where I was meant to be. Over time, I grew in my role and developed a deep understanding of the intricacies of human resources. This experience laid the foundation for my future career advancements.

New opportunities emerged as I continued to trust God and allow Him to guide my path. I transitioned into various human resources roles, each building upon the last. With each step, I gained valuable skills and insights that prepared me for my current position as a C-Suite executive.

Looking back, I am grateful for the journey and the lessons learned along the way. God's plan was far greater than anything I could have envisioned for myself. My initial disappointment and uncertainty were transformed into opportunities for growth and advancement.

Today, I strive to live by the principle of trusting God's timing and plan. When faced with challenges and setbacks, I remind myself that He is still writing my story. I no longer feel the need to control every aspect of my life or to have all the answers. Instead, I focus on being patient and faithful, knowing that God's plan is unfolding perfectly.

In my current role, I carry with me the lessons learned from my journey. I approach my work with a sense of purpose and humility, understanding that my career is not just about personal success but about making a positive impact on others. I strive to lead with integrity and compassion, drawing on the experiences that have shaped me.

My story is a testament to the power of faith and the importance of trusting God's plan. It is a reminder that our lives are not defined by a single moment or achievement but by the journey we undertake and the faith we hold onto along the way.

When I encounter others who are facing their own struggles and uncertainties, I share my story and the wisdom that has guided me: Please be patient with yourself; God is not through with you yet. He is still writing your story, and it's important to trust Him and His timing. Life's purpose and fulfillment are not achieved in a day but through a series of steps guided by His hand.

My journey has shown me that every experience, whether joyous or challenging, is part of a larger plan. By surrendering control and trusting in God, I have found a sense of peace and direction. I no longer feel the need to rush or to force outcomes. Instead, I embrace each day as an opportunity to grow and move closer to the purpose God has for me.

As I continue on this path, I remain open to the lessons and opportunities that lie ahead. I know that God is still at work in my life, crafting my story with care and precision. With each new chapter, I trust that His plan is unfolding perfectly, and I look forward to the future with hope and faith.

In conclusion, please be patient with me. God is not through with me yet. This simple yet profound truth has been a guiding light in my life. I have experienced growth, fulfillment, and purpose beyond my wildest dreams by trusting God and allowing Him to write my story. My journey serves as a testament to the power of faith and the importance of surrendering to God's plan.

Grandma Vernesta's Words of Wisdom on Evolving:
"Trust in God to order your steps."

Reflect on Your Growth Journey:

- Reflect on a situation where you had to trust the Lord with all your heart, even when it didn't make sense. How did leaning not on your own understanding help you navigate this situation? Write about the outcome and how your faith was strengthened through this experience.

- Describe what it looks like for you to submit to God in all your ways on a daily basis. How do you incorporate this submission into your routine and decision-making processes? Write about the changes you've noticed in your life when you consistently submit to Him.

- Think about a time when you faced uncertainty or confusion. How did the scripture, "lean not on your own understanding," guide you through this period? Reflect on how trusting God's wisdom over your own provided clarity and direction.

- Write about a "path-making" moment in your life when you felt God was directly making your path straight. What steps did you take to trust and submit to Him during this time? How did this experience affirm your faith and trust in God's guidance?

- Reflect on how you can strengthen your trust in the Lord and improve your ability to submit to Him in all your ways. What spiritual practices, such as prayer, reading scripture, or worship, help you rely more on God's understanding rather than your own? Write about the impact these practices have on your faith journey.

- Congratulations! You are one step closer to leading a rewarding life! Where do you go from here? After reading this book, you may feel inspired and ready to make changes in your life. Remember, transformation begins with you, and believing in yourself is crucial to this journey. Here are some practical next steps to help you integrate the book's teachings into your daily life:

- **Reflect on Key Takeaways:**

Begin by reflecting on the insights that resonated most with you. Take notes on the chapters that sparked your interest or felt particularly relevant. Use the questions in the Reflect on Your Journey to deepen your understanding and help clarify how they apply to your life.

- **Set Personal Goals**

Using the insights you've gained, set specific and achievable personal goals. Consider areas where you'd like to grow spiritually or emotionally. For example, you might aim to cultivate more gratitude, enhance mindfulness, or improve your relationships. Write these goals down, breaking them into smaller, actionable steps that you can incorporate into your daily routine.

- **Create Daily Practices**

Establish daily practices that align with the book's teachings. These could include meditation, prayer, journaling, or reading spiritual texts. Consistency is key, so start with manageable practices that you can realistically maintain. Over time, these habits will help reinforce your spiritual growth and keep you connected to the book's lessons.

- **Join a Community**

Consider joining a group or community that shares your spiritual interests. Engaging with like-minded individuals provides support, encouragement, and accountability. Whether it's a meditation group, a book club, or an online forum, being part of a community can enhance your spiritual journey and offer new perspectives.

- **Apply Lessons to Real-Life**

Identify specific areas of your life where you can apply the teachings. This might involve changing your response to challenges, practicing forgiveness, or adopting a more mindful approach to daily activities. Actively integrating these lessons into your life will help solidify the changes you aim to make

- **Monitor Your Progress**

Regularly assess your progress toward your goals. Reflect on what's working well and where you might need to adjust your approach. Celebrate your successes, no matter how small, and view setbacks as opportunities for learning and growth. Remember, progress is not always linear, and self-compassion is essential.

- **Seek Further Learning**

Continue your journey by exploring additional resources that align with your spiritual path. This might include other books, podcasts, workshops, or retreats. Continuous learning can deepen your understanding and reinforce your commitment to personal development.

- **Practice Self-Compassion**

Be kind to yourself throughout this process. Personal growth takes time, and it's important to practice self-compassion when you encounter challenges. Recognize that setbacks are a natural part of the journey, and they provide valuable lessons that contribute to your growth.

- **Share Your Journey**

If comfortable, share your insights and progress with others. Discussing your experiences can reinforce your understanding and inspire others on similar paths. Sharing also fosters connection and community, which are vital components of spiritual growth.

- **Stay Open to Change**

Finally, remain open to evolving your beliefs and practices. Spiritual development is a dynamic process, and it's important to be flexible and receptive to new ideas and experiences. Your needs and understanding may change as you grow, and that's perfectly okay.

ABOUT THE AUTHOR

Crystal's journey is a testament to her unwavering commitment to helping others thrive professionally and personally. As an Executive Human Resources Professional and a Master Certified Life Coach, she has dedicated her career to fostering environments where individuals can achieve their fullest potential. Her love for people is evident in every aspect of her work and personal life, reflecting a deep-seated passion for nurturing spiritual and physical well-being that began in her early years.

Born and raised in Fayetteville, North Carolina, Crystal's upbringing played a significant role in shaping her values and aspirations. Being raised in a close-knit community, she was surrounded by family and friends who emphasized the importance of compassion, integrity, and perseverance. These early influences ignited a love for helping others, setting the stage for her future endeavors.

After completing her education, Crystal embarked on a career in human resources, quickly rising through the ranks due to her exceptional leadership abilities and innate understanding of people. Her expertise in Human Resources was not just limited to administrative tasks; she excelled in creating inclusive workplaces where employees felt valued and motivated. Crystal's approach to human resources was holistic, recognizing that employees' well-being was integral to their productivity and job satisfaction.

Crystal's dedication to physical well-being is equally strong. She advocates for a balanced lifestyle that includes regular exercise, healthy eating, and adequate rest. She often shares tips and resources with her clients to help them adopt healthier habits and routines. Crystal's own life is a testament to the benefits of this holistic approach; she maintains a rigorous fitness routine and prioritizes her physical health alongside her spiritual and emotional well-being.

Despite her demanding career, Crystal has always made time for her family. She now lives in Loudoun County, Virginia, with her two children, who are the light of her life. Balancing her professional responsibilities with her role as a mother has not always been easy. Still, Crystal approaches this challenge with the same dedication and love that she brings to her work.

She strives to be a positive role model for her children, teaching them the importance of kindness, resilience, and self-belief.

Crystal has found a community that shares her values and passions. She actively participates in local initiatives promoting well-being, education, and community development. Her contributions have earned her the respect and admiration of her peers, and she continues to inspire others with her unwavering commitment to making a difference. Crystal is an active member of Delta Sigma Theta Sorority, Incorporated, The Links Incorporated, Reston (VA) Chapter, The 12 Days of Christmas, Loudoun Chapter, and The Loudoun County Virginia Chapter of Jack and Jill of America.

Crystal remains a beacon of positivity and strength. She embodies the principles of compassion, integrity, and excellence, always striving to uplift those around her. Her journey is a testament to the power of faith, perseverance, and a heart dedicated to serving others. Through her work and her life, Crystal continues to inspire, empower, and make a lasting impact on the world around her.

Made in the USA
Columbia, SC
20 September 2024

42663692R10102